W9-AFO-354

LOMBARDI.

"I've been written up as a beast, as a lot of things. I don't know what I am."

LOMBARDI.

Edited by

John Wiebusch

Epilogue by

James Dickey

Photography by

Vernon Biever

An Officially Licensed Publication of the National Football League

Reproduced and reprinted in 1997 by Triumph Books, Chicago, Illinois.

This book is available in quantity at special discounts for your group or organization. For further information, contact:

Triumph Books
644 South Clark Street
Chicago, Illinois 60605
(312) 939-3330 FAX (312) 663-3557

FIRST 1997 EDITION
1 2 3 4 5 6 7 8 9 10

ISBN 1-57243-028-1

Printed in the United States of America

Contents

Prologue

Thirty NFL seasons have passed since he last was carried off the field on the shoulders of his players after Super Bowl II in Miami.

Twenty-seven NFL seasons have gone by since cancer claimed him at age 57 on September 3, 1970.

And yet the legend and legacy of Vincent Thomas Lombardi is as alive as if it were yesterday.

He was the Packers' coach for nine seasons and his teams were kings of the NFL hill five times. He won the first two Super Bowls (back before the game was called that) and the piece of silver that goes to pro football's best team is called the Vince Lombardi Trophy. He was elected to the Pro Football Hall of Fame four months after he died.

This book about him was first published in 1971. It disappeared from regular bookstores and was not reprinted. For more than a quarter-century, you could find it only in rare bookstores.

Except for the words on this page and updated legal copy, it is reproduced exactly—and lovingly—as it was then.

Flip ahead to the photograph on page 14.

Here's looking at you, Coach.

John Wiebusch
June 15, 1997

Looking through a program. Flipping the pages from the back during a timeout. Stopping at a picture of the coaching staff of the Green Bay Packers. There, front center, squinting into the sun. Him. Vince Lombardi. And that funny mouth of his.

I always thought he had a funny mouth. All that space between the teeth. Those big teeth. I thought when he laughed he would look like something in the front window on Halloween. If I would *see* him laugh. I thought when he snarled – I knew he would – he would look like something swimming up on Lloyd Bridges, a fin sticking out of the water. I thought of stalagmites and stalactites and the MGM lion.

Me, knowing I would have to talk to him later, talking to myself. Mostly to myself. Saying, God, please let the Packers win this one. Oh God, one favor. Let the Packers win this one and I'll never ask for anything else again because I don't think I can go down there and face him if they lose.

Saying, then, you big dumb phony. Saying to myself that I *couldn't* want the Green Bay Packers to win. No way. Hating the Green Bay Packers. Always hating them. Glancing back down at the program. At the MGM lion. Me, speaking to no one and everyone, "C'mon, Joe Baby. Let's get us going here." Big dumb phony. Noticing the guy next to me and his clenched fists on the table. Knowing he wanted Joe Baby to get us going, too, and hearing him say, "Yeah," grimly. Someone else saying, "Kapp'll choke. Watch. The apple." A voice, coming from the second row. Or down on the other end of the pressbox. From somewhere. Me, saying, "Bull," softly, and, once more, "C'mon, Joe Baby." Big dumb phony.

Then reason. For a moment. This game means nothing to the Vikings. Three games they've won all year. Three. It means nothing. Some face saving, maybe. A little confidence for next year. Some pride. A *little* pride. What the hell else? The Vikings can win this game and they're still going to finish last and I'm going to get my head snapped off by Vince Lombardi. Me, I'm going to have to suffer because the Vikings who are going to finish last anyway are going to win a lousy game that means nothing to them.

Thinking of how it will be.

Oh God.

The questions...

"Do you think your team let down after winning the title last week?"

"Do you think you lose an edge when you win a championship three weeks before the end of the season?"

Glares. Those eyes. Looking daggers.

"Coach, John Wiebusch. Minneapolis Tribune."

Should I have said Coach Lombardi or Mr. Lombardi? Or Vince? Or Vinnie? Naw, not after a loss. Coach. That's it.

"... Minneapolis Tribune." Stuttering.

Those eyes. Saying, who really gives a damn?

More questions.

"Can the Vikings be a contender next year?"

"Do you think you can come back against the Rams next week?"

"Would you rather face Los Angeles or Baltimore in the playoffs?"

Snarl. No reply. Only a go-to-hell snarl.

Leaving the locker room and saying, my God, I have no story. I am no match for this man and I have no story. Thinking of what I will say upstairs. "That goddamn son of a bitch gave me nothing." Sympathy. Knowing that I'll get sympathy because they know how he is. "Doesn't surprise me." "He's a mean S.O.B." Me, nodding, and saying, "I tried. I got nothing from him but I tried."

Jolted by the noise of the crowd, the rickety clatter of Metropolitan Stadium. Lousy goddamn Vikings. Win this game and you're still going to finish last. Four teams. Fourth place. A disgrace.

In the third quarter. Vikings 17, Packers 13. Then, a miracle. Bart Starr throwing a football and Carroll Dale pulling it out of the air for a touchdown. The Packers are in front. Then another touchdown. Ben Wilson barging across from the 1. Is *Ben Wilson* really a Green Bay Packer? Really? Packers 27, Vikings 17. Nothing to worry about.

Through the glasses, Lombardi moving on the sidelines. The man who has the glasses saying, "A 10-point lead and he can't even smile." Not smiling? With a lead like that? He *has* to be smiling. Me, saying, "Let me see those glasses." Scanning the hashmarks. Finding him, on the 40. In a big brown coat. His arms at his sides. Yelling something and looking like hell hath no fury. My God!

In the fourth quarter. The corpse begins to move. The Vikings are moving, behind Joe Baby. A touchdown first and then a field goal. Packers 27, Vikings 27. Fists pounding on the table beside me and silence in the second row. Jeez, what a comeback! Watching him without the glasses. Pacing. No, stalking. His face contorted. Knowing it *must* be contorted. Reaching for the glasses. Finding him instantly, there with his contorted face and his angry mouth.

Saying, "Is this some kind of game?," and knowing that afterwards it is going to be awful down there. Damn him. Damn them. Damn everybody.

Remembering...

Remembering how it was the first time I had to talk to Mickey Mantle. Scared. Remembering how I never really thought about it that time until I stood behind him, waiting for him to turn around. Then, saying, "Mickey, John Wiebusch. Minneapolis Tribune," and thinking in the same moment, hey, what the hell is this? What the hell am *I* doing talking to Mickey Mantle? Absolute stark raving terror. Wanting, at that moment, to run.

And now Lombardi.

Late in the game. The Vikings have the ball. They've had it this whole quarter. It seems that way. Time, there is time, and all it will take is a field goal. Momentum. Joe Baby running, scrambling. A meeting of bodies. A fumble. Tom Brown atop it at the 28. Lucky. Lucky Tom Brown. Lucky Green Bay Packers. Always they have been lucky. Always under Lombardi. I hate that team. I always have.

Remembering then who I wanted to win. Who my *head* wanted to win. Sometimes my heart overwhelms my head. The Packers can win now. All Chandler has to do is kick a field goal. Happy ending. Happy Lombardi.

Eight seconds left on the clock. Bart Starr kneeling at the 19 and taking the snap and putting it down for Don Chandler. The kick. The upstretched arms. Finally, Packers 30, Vikings 27. Incredible.

Grabbing notebooks and play-by-plays. Running for the elevator. More concerned now with getting through the crowd than with what will follow. "Hey, hold that thing for me!" Down to the basement and up the corridor to the left. A vendor, passing the other way, mad. "What a lousy way to lose." Yeah. On to the locker room. A guard there, in front of the door. "Just a few minutes, fellows." More time to think. Unwanted time to think. God, at least there are six of us. No, seven. I couldn't have faced him alone. Win or lose. No way. Emerging from the door, a head. The guard, nodding and smiling. "Okay, fellows." Moving through the door. Through a short passage. Through another door. In the locker room. Waiting for the group to gather around Lombardi. Getting in behind them. Waiting for him to finish unlacing his boots and look up.

Then, suddenly, "What's on your mind?"

Nervous shuffling in the group. Someone says, "Quite a finish, huh?"

No response. Lombardi pulls off the left boot.

Someone asks, "Were you ready to settle for a tie?"

Lombardi looks up. He says, "I'm never ready to settle for a tie."

Someone says, "That Tom Brown, he just keeps making the big plays."

Lombardi is unbuttoning his thermal underwear. He says, "Tom Brown's quite a football player."

More questions. More short answers. Mostly short answers. Me, scribbling notes on my pad. Forgetting about my intimidator.

Then, "That all, gentlemen?"

Someone says, "Yeah, thanks, coach," and Lombardi gets off his stool and trudges toward the shower.

Thinking, it could have been better but it could have been worse. God knows it could have been worse. A tough game for him. A drain on his emotions. Figuring that and figuring we got off easy, all of us. Especially me. All the while I said just one word. Only, "Thanks," when he moved past me when it was over. Just one muttered word.

I know him now. I met him . . . well, I met him in a lot of places.

. . . in an apartment on the North Side of Chicago, a block up from the lake. Paul Hornung smoked cigarettes and drank beer. He had his bare feet up on the coffee table. When the telephone rang for the fourth time he said, "Damn telephone."

. . . at the side of a pool in Miami Beach. Wellington Mara sat in the shade of the cabana, his face a mottled red. He said, "I keep expecting to see him come out of that door."

. . . in a room of rosewood in Palm Desert, California. I told Col. Blaik he looked like Gen. MacArthur. He liked that.

. . . in a noisy quick-food restaurant in Los Angeles. Boyd Dowler arrived 15 minutes late. I said, "In Green Bay you're *30* minutes late." Boyd laughed.

. . . in a bar across the East River from Yankee Stadium, on the fringe of Harlem. Emlen Tunnell said, "I could sit here and talk for days." I said, "I'll bet you could."

. . . in an office eight flights up in Minneapolis. Vince Lombardi, Jr., talked about life with his father. He said, "I might get pretty emotional about some of the stuff I'm going to tell you." The air conditioner was loud.

. . . in the front room of a sprawling house on the rolling green of the Maryland countryside. Marie Lombardi turned the pages of an album that contained pictures of her grandchildren. "They'll never know him," she said and she began to weep.

I know him now. I really do.
I wish there were more I could say than, "Thanks."

John Wiebusch
April 2, 1971

Moods

“Dancing is a contact sport. Football is a collision sport.”

"The new leadership is in sacrifice, is in self-denial. It is in love, it is in fearlessness. It is in humility and it is in the perfectly disciplined will. This is also the distinction between great and little men."

Moods: the man of many faces

WELLINGTON MARA: If you said good morning to him in the right way you could bring tears to his eyes.

JIM LEE HOWELL: His emotions were something. He had so many peaks and valleys the guys started calling him "Hi-Low."

ART ROONEY: I asked him to send a card to Tim Kiely, a 10-year-old friend who was a grade school football candidate. He thought awhile and then wrote: "Dear Tim: If you want to make St. Bede's football team, you must be mentally tough. Best, Vince Lombardi."

FATHER DAVID RONDOU: I'd see him come in that side door, always a little grin on his face, and I'd think, by golly, with all the worries and problems and difficulties of being head coach for so many years and, here, he could be so personal. I'll remember that smile, when I'd see him in the morning.

TEX SCHRAMM: They had a room at Mona Kai that was on the ocean and he loved to watch the sun go down. Damn near every night the phone would ring in our room and he'd say, "You'd better get up here. Get up here. Hurry up." And so we'd get up there and we'd just sit there, watching the sunset.

JERRY GREEN: When he came into the Royal Hawaiian before the meeting there in March he was wearing a lei around his neck and he was grinning. Suddenly he became aware that he was out of character. You could see it. He carefully removed the lei and handed it to Marie.

JIM FINKS: It's funny to think so but when you met him for the first time he'd give you a dead-fish handshake and he'd avoid contact with your eyes. When he trusted you it was just the opposite.

ETHEL KENNEDY: It was in late May of 1969 and Ben and Toni Bradlee – he's the editor of the Washington Post – were giving a surprise birthday party for Edward Bennett Williams. As I walked in the Bradlee's garden, the first thing I noticed were several large photographic blowups of Ed and former Redskin coaches. I remember two pictures in particular. One was of Ed with his arm around Bill McPeak and the cartoon balloon over Ed's head had him saying. "Don't worry, Bill. I'll always stand behind you." The other was a large blowup of Otto Graham and Ed. They seemed to be studying blueprints and Ed was saying, "Otto, are you sure you want to build a house in Washington?" I wondered how Coach Lombardi felt when he saw the pictures. We soon found out. In his cryptic toast to Ed after dinner he barked, "I can assure you of one thing, Ed. My photograph will never be hanging from one of those trees."

This was one of the first nights I had gone out and I was thinking of just saying hello to everyone and then disappearing after cocktails. But Art Buchwald said, "We rigged it so you'll be sitting next to the Coach." That sinking feeling! Then we were propelled into the dining room. The moment we sat down and he turned to speak to me I knew that everything would be all right. He was so warm and sympathetic and enthusiastic. He told me how he had first met President Kennedy and then Bobby, and how much they meant to him and how they had the same qualities which made great athletes. He said everything I wanted to hear. While he was talking I said a prayer of thanks to Bobby for organizing it so that I would be asked to the party and, best of all, be seated next to Vince. I asked the Coach if he would take an active role in getting the NFL involved in teaching football to underprivileged kids. He was familiar with the successful New York Giants program and he said, "Just give me a few months to get the Redskins in shape and then I'll head it up." He was a man of few words but he never said anything he didn't mean. I'm sure had he lived the program would be going strong.

He was like a rock. Everything in his philosophy and his life reaffirmed all my childhood beliefs. Seated next to me was a man – with that marvelously toothy grin – who was expounding on the need for competition, desire, drive, discipline and pride. I remember thinking this is how a mountain climber must feel when he reaches the protective overhang of a rock. Always the image of a rock – and then it clicked . . . one of the Seven Blocks of Granite. His presence was so overwhelming I forgot who else was in the room – except for one other person, Marie. The conversation at our table came around to Vince's toughness. Much to my surprise, from about six seats away, Marie's penetrating voice shot across the table: "Everyone thinks Vince is fierce. hardboiled, temperamental and ruthless – when in truth he's just a bunny!" I asked Vince if he thought that particular image of him occurred to his players. He said he didn't think so.

He was tough, we all knew that, and as we talked I hated to think what was in store for Sonny Jurgensen's tummy, not to mention what he planned for the rest of the team. I asked him who were the five best players he had coached and he said Doc Blanchard, Frank Gifford, Bart Starr and Sonny Jurgensen. The fifth is probably better left nameless. He knows who he is but in Vince's time he coached so many greats that it's probably better to let them keep their dreams.

Vince was his own man – as I found out later in the evening. I was hoping he could come to New York for a benefit the following Monday and I asked Ed Williams to try to bring Vince and Marie with him. Ed put his arm around Vince and said, "Oh sure, the Coach will come to New York on Monday." Vince just grinned and said clearly and distinctly, "Yes, Vince would love to come to New York on Monday, but Vince is going to be in Washington on Monday looking at some of the worst football films he has ever seen."

JIMMY CANNON: There was no way you could have agreed with Vinnie completely. If you had, there would have been no reason for him to exist.

TOM LANDRY: He never compromised. There was one way and that was his.

FATHER KEVIN O'BRIEN: His toughness should not be equated to rigidity but to stability.

PAUL MAZZOLENI: One day at practice Paul Hornung kicked a field goal and the ball sailed over the fence. A boy got the ball and raced for home only to be caught by another boy, who took the ball away from the other kid and brought it back. The boy ran on the field to give the ball to Lombardi but when Lombardi saw the lad he was mad and he told the police to get the kid off the field. Vince put up quite a fuss. After practice, the officer explained why the boy got on the field and he told Lombardi how proud the boy had been to get the ball back. Lombardi felt badly and told the officer to find the boy. For four days, Lombardi would ask the officer if he had found the boy yet. He hadn't. On the fifth day the boy came around. Lombardi hadn't forgotten. He jostled the boy's hair, thanked him and gave him a football.

ZEKE BRATKOWSKI: Playing golf with him was a great experience. Once I came to the last hole and he and I were partners and I had about a 3½-foot putt to win for us. And he said, "You'd better make that." He didn't put any pressure on me! So I made the putt and we beat Jerry Kramer and Max McGee. But I wonder what would have happened if I had missed it!

TEX SCHRAMM: He and I were partners. It was the two of us against Paul Brown and Mark Duncan. And Lombardi and Brown had a side bet, too. Ooh, Vince wanted to win that one! And after seven holes on the front nine he's up by two and then on the eighth hole he misses a short putt – that would have given him a halve – and he's mad, of course. Then just as he's about to get into the cart, a ball came from somewhere on the left and hit him on the head. Not hard. It bounced first or it might have hurt him badly. But it stung anyway. Now Vince wasn't in a good frame of mind with that missed putt and all and as he starts up the fairway he's swinging his putter and calling the guy who had hit into him every name in the book. That voice just echoed everywhere and of course the other guy heard it. Vince was so upset that he also blew the ninth hole to push the front side. He was boiling. Then on the back side, after two, three holes, we're waiting at a short par three when the group in back of us caught up. It was this guy and two other guys and a woman. The guy hands Vince a club and he says, "I think this is your wedge. You threw it back there," and Vince nods and says, "Thanks." Then the guy says, "I want to apologize for hitting into you," and Vince grunts and say, "Okay, fine. Forget it," and the guy says, "But I want to say that there was no excuse for the vulgar language you used in front of this lady." Well, you could see the blood rush to Vince's head and he was off again, chewing this guy up and down. Then he stepped up and really hooked an iron shot. Now three holes after that, like on 16 or 17 or so, someone looks back and says, "Here comes that guy again," and damned if he hasn't got the same wedge again. Vince would toss clubs now and then. And the guy says, "We accept your apology for everything

Ockie Krueger Earl Blaik

that's happened today," and Vince throws his arms in the air and says, "They accept my apology? My God!" This same guy is going to play golf again the next day and he asks at the desk when Lombardi's playing because he doesn't want to be near him again and they say that Mr. Lombardi always plays in the afternoon. So he gets a morning tee-off. Guess who joined the foursome just ahead of him? Vince had to laugh and so did the guy. They were compatible that day.

PAUL BROWN: Vince was hopping mad that day in Hawaii. Some guy hit him in the head with a golf ball and that just took care of his day. Every time I'd mention the incident to him he'd knock the ball 50 yards straight up in the air! Every time! That's probably the reason I beat him.

MARK DUNCAN: I don't think Vince Lombardi and Paul Brown ever played golf together as partners. They always played *against* each other. It was interesting because here are two guys and neither one of them ever wanted to lose.

HOWARD COSELL: I'm a superb gin player. He didn't think he was bad but I'm watching him and he's beginning to lose. He knows I've got a photographic mind and he's getting increasingly disturbed. So the other guy gins and Vince turns around and says, "Goddammit will you get the hell over to the bar and have a drink? I can't stand having you watch me. I know what you're thinking." I just roared. And I threw that incident up to him for the rest of his life. He just couldn't stand being seen in an area where he wasn't the best. He couldn't stand it. So every time I'd see him I'd say, "Hey, Vince, you wanna play a round of gin?"

BILL FORESTER: During the exhibition season one year we stayed for a week on a college campus in Washington. There was a pool room in the basement of the dormitory and coach'd hurry over there after practice looking for a game. He'd be as frisky as he could be in that pool room. Like he knew he was gonna win. And then Max McGee or one of the other sharks would beat him and he would go storming out. The next night he'd return, frisky and ready. Mostly, those nights ended with him storming out mad.

FRANK COWLES: He felt that he could have won every game he coached.

STORMY BIDWILL: We were in an airplane coming back from the funeral of Vic Morabito, the owner of the 49ers. On the plane, Vince was quite talkative

and loose about many things, including football, when a man came up and introduced himself, said he was from somewhere in Wisconsin and congratulated Vince on the previous year. Vince immediately squeezed down in his seat and stayed there for quite some time before he loosened up again.

LEE REMMEL: We went out for dinner with him after this really close game that the Packers had won. A man came over to the table and he knelt down by Lombardi. You could see the guy was pretty well in his cups. He said to the coach, "I consider you next to Jesus Christ." Lombardi was terribly embarrassed. It was awful until the guy left.

MORRIS SIEGEL: He loved people, but only his kind of people. When he attended a party at Sardi's after the opening of "Sheep on the Runway" in New York, he was fawned over by the contrived, pretentious people. He smiled grimly and then he tugged on the sleeve of a friend and said, "These aren't my people. Let's get the hell out of here." So four of us wound up in the back room of a Third Avenue saloon, where Lombardi opened his tie and felt comfortable for the first time since leaving the theater. From there we went to a late-hours Irish pub on Lombardi's recommendation. "I haven't been here in a helluva long time," he said, "but it used to be a good, fun spot." It was. And Lombardi accompanied the band as a volunteer soloist on some Italian and Irish numbers. He even danced with a reporter, Myra MacPherson of the Washington Post. I said to him, "I've never seen you like this," and he said, "This is the off-season for me."

BILL AUSTIN: He wanted to have fun but he didn't want many people to see him enjoying himself. Only his closest friends ever saw him let the barriers down.

EDWARD BENNETT WILLIAMS: Basically, he was kind of an insecure man, you know.

BILL AUSTIN: He used to smoke like a fiend. He was writing on the blackboard in front of the team and he turned around to take a drag on his cigarette. He put the chalk in his mouth instead and then he smashed it down on the floor.

JACK TEELE: I was working on the Pro Bowl and Vince was the Western club's coach. It was after the game and he was giving an interview to the press and I was sitting next to him. I looked back on the fringe and there was a guy standing there I didn't recognize and I thought to myself, gee, I probably should get up and go back and check that guy's credentials. And just at that moment, just then, Lombardi nudged me and said, "Who is that guy in back?" And I said, "I don't know coach," so he said, "Excuse me, gentlemen," and he yelled out, "Hey you, you in back there. Are you a member of the press?" And the guy said "No,"and Vince said,"Are you with radio or TV?" And the guy said, "No," and Vince said, "Well you get your ass out of here!" The guy turned around and walked out. No one *ever* challenged his authority.

PAUL MAZZOLENI: He had made arrangements to practice and house the team at St. Norbert and a truck was needed to haul films and records to the college. So Jack Vanisi, his talent scout, asked me to help in the moving. I ran a service station and my truck was just what they needed. It was a hot day, around 90, and boy!, those boxes were heavy. As I was unloading the boxes at the college, Lombardi was telling me where to put them. I finished the job around noon and Jack told me to stick around and have lunch with the players. I was waiting in the hallway for Jack and as I was waiting Lombardi walked by and drilled a look at me. He said, "What are you hanging around for?" My reply was, "I was just leaving, sir." I left then. The next day Lombardi called me and bawled me out for not speaking up to him. He thanked me then.

SAM HUFF: He wanted you to stand up to him, to fight back. When he'd get mad at someone he'd go back in his office and he'd say, "I wish the son of a bitch would stand up and say what he thinks!" Very few people ever took him up on his offer.

EARL BLAIK: His volatile temper was the very thing that made him great. I realized that later. On his first day of football practice at West Point, I called him aside to talk to him about something and while he was with me his group engaged in a little horseplay. He pivoted away from me and toward them and he was swearing and yelling. I called him back right then and I told him that that kind of thing didn't go at the Academy. It was the last time I ever talked to him about his temper.

MIKE MANUCHE: Vinnie had his faults. He said himself, "I'm selfish." He wanted things his way. He had a violent temper and he knew that was a fault. He said lots of times, "I did something I'm sorry for." He felt like all men who devote a lot of time to their business that he didn't spend enough time with his family. He considered that a fault, too.

VINCE LOMBARDI, JR.: With me he was pretty free with the back of his hand but five minutes later it would be forgotten. I think all that anger bit is overplayed. I remember lots of times him being in a great mood before he had to go in and talk to somebody. He wouldn't have had any stomach left if he were as acid as they said he was. But he could turn it on or off, no question about it.

Once he started rolling it was the real thing. I think he had a knack of letting little things bother him. It didn't take a crisis for him to get going. I think he even looked for the little things. Sometimes he'd come home from the office and forget where he was. That's when my mother put her foot down.

But my father and I really had some classic blowouts, no question. He'd never say, "I think it's raining. You'd better wear your boots." He'd say, "Get out of here with your boots on."

The last really big thing we had was back in New Jersey. I slammed the door and he came out after me and I hit him. He'd been on me for quite some time and I just hit him before he did anything to me. He was really shocked. He went back into the house and he came out and he was ready to do me in. He wouldn't have knocked me down, only cuffed me. And my mother was really trying to keep him away and I could hear the shuffling of feet and my father saying, "Get out of the way, let me at him!," and my mother saying "Oh no, remember what you did to him last time."

And then there were the times when I'd really do something wrong – get thrown out of school or something. I'd worry about it all day, that I'd have to come home and tell him that I got thrown out of school. Then he'd come in and talk about it and he always seemed to know when the time was not to be physical about things.

TEX SCHRAMM: My recollections of him are not the normal fiery, driving, emotional type. My recollections of him are very sentimental, pleasant warm ones. And that's not a picture that was painted to the public.

MARIE LOMBARDI: It's not true that he did all the interior decorating of his Packer offices. They said how he picked out the color of the carpet and the color of the paint and the drapes. That just wasn't true. There was an interior designer hired to do those things and I'll never forget walking into his office when it was done and seeing drapes on the windows with horses on them. I said, "What is this, a jockey club or a football coach's office?"

Not many people knew it but he was colorblind. He could tell green from red or orange from brown but he had trouble with shadings, subtleties. He'd come downstairs in the morning and look at me and say, "What do you think?," and I'd say, "Well, you've got red brown and green brown on and they don't mix." He'd get mad and I'd tell him he'd asked for an opinion and he'd gotten it. "Go on, get out of here," I'd say. "If you want to look like a fool go right ahead." Once in a while he'd change.

CHUCK LANE: One spring I was over in Minneapolis playing rugby. I'd go there on weekends. I really got banged up that afternoon – rugby's a very physical sport – and I ended up in the hospital. It was obvious I wasn't going to be able to get back to Green Bay for work on Monday. It was the off-season and there wasn't that much pressing business in the office anyway. But I knew Lombardi wanted me to be there and so I called him on Monday morning from my hospital bed and I explained that the doctor was not going to release me for four days and that I'd have to take a few days off. The reaction on the other end of the line was that of an explosion. He's screaming and hollering and carrying on and he told me, "You damn well better get back here because all the time you spend in the hospital's going to come off your vacation!" I wanted to come back right then but they wouldn't let me go until Wednesday. I stormed into his office and I was just as livid as he had been on the phone Monday. I said, "I'm upset and disappointed." And he just sat there and bellowed with laughter. He just wanted to see how far he could push me.

JIM FINKS: In my first year with the Vikings we'd done some signing things with a couple of football players from Oklahoma, Lance Rentzel and Jim Grisham, that violated league rules. So there was a national conference call and each club representative spoke his mind and suggested various punishments. I was petrified when it came to Lombardi because I'd never even met the man, only heard about him. When it was his turn he said, "I think it was an immature act by some immature people. Let's let it go at that."

WELLINGTON MARA: We'd always talked about Europe but it was never more than that. But after the 1962 season we did it and it was off to Rome and Vinnie's homeland. The first time in a restaurant was wonderful. Vince couldn't speak or read Italian but he insisted he could, more out of pride than anything,

I guess. Marie wanted this beef dish and she was about to order it from the waiter when Vinnie said, "Listen, will you please let me order?" So he ordered for the two of them. Well, Marie ended up getting roast pork and Vince had to laugh. He said, "What the hell do I know about Italian?"

¶ On the plane coming back, Vinnie and Marie sat in front of us and we're filling out our customs reports. First of all, you must know that Vinnie was impeccably honest. Marie, well, Marie's like the rest of us, a thing or two hidden away in the suitcase here and there. So they finished with the customs card and Marie starts feeling guilty and she tells him about something she "forgot". He tore up the card and started over. This must have happened five or six times and at that point the hairs on the back of his neck literally were standing on end.

¶ Another time they were in Puerto Rico and when it was time to come home they decided that a special rum bottle would be a nice decorative item. It still was about a quarter full, though, so they wrapped it in a towel from the Dorado Beach Hotel. This was during a period when the customs people really were cracking down and so when he came through they asked him to open his bags. Right there on top was the big Dorado Beach Hotel towel. He was mortified. Naturally everyone around them knew who he was. And then the customs man says they owe 40 cents duty or something like that on the rum and now he's a wildman. "Take the goddamned stuff," he said. "I don't want it!"

JIM FINKS: Two stories he loved to tell on himself. One was about filling out a customs report when they came back from Europe and the other was about a bottle of rum they brought back from Puerto Rico. God, how he would laugh!

RAY NITSCHKE: He had a hard exterior but he also had a big, soft heart.

DAVE SLATTERY: The first trip we took with him in Washington, we were flying out of Homestead Air Force Base outside of Harrisburg, Pa. The first thing that happened, it hadn't happened in 10 or 15 years – the equipment truck broke down. So he's screaming about that and he's screaming at me for not having the equipment men ride the truck. Well, at this point I could've said – what could they have done? – but this was not the spot to argue. So after a delay, the players were getting on the plane and they're jockeying for seats. He and Mrs. Lombardi always took the left-rear seat in the forward compartment of a 727. And he yelled for me and I finally worked my way back to him. I had Joe Marshall with me, who was my student assistant at the time. And Lombardi just stuck his head out and roared down the rear compartment of the plane, "Goddammit, sit down!" And everybody fell over. Marshall knocked me right into the seat. And Lombardi turned around to me and said, "Not you, you damn fool!" I had one foot stuck up in the air. And then he shook his head and said, "No wonder they can't win. They don't know when to sit down and they don't know when to stand up."

BART STARR: He was tough and abusive and at times he was downright nasty.

OCKIE KRUEGER: He and Marie were coming down to Milwaukee to meet me and my wife on the occasion of a birthday or anniversary. He said they'd meet us at 5:30 at this hotel in Milwaukee. "Fine," I said. "You leave Green Bay at 3:30 and we'll see you there at 5:30." Well, I know all about Lombardi time and so I said to my wife, "We'll get there at a quarter to 5 and we'll wait in the lobby because he's gonna come storming in there about 10 minutes to 5 and wonder where we are." So we get ready and we're just about to leave the house at 4:15 – it only takes 10 minutes to drive downtown – when the phone rang and this voice said very loudly, "Where are you?" Well, he got in hysterics on the other end and I got in hysterics, too. This was at 4:15 for a 5:30 date!

DICK BOURGUIGNON: There would be about six or eight people sitting around and he would bring up something controversial and someone would say, "Wait a while, Vince, I don't agree with you on that," and he'd push the issue and pretty soon he'd have everybody arguing and then the son of a bitch would just sit back there and grin while everybody was arguing the point. I'd catch him doing that. But you could work it just the opposite. Like I'd say something and then I'd wink at Marie and, ooh, he'd get excited. He'd blow his stack and all of a sudden he'd realize he had been sucked in. And we would all be laughing.

ZEKE BRATKOWSKI: Nobody ever laughed when he talked unless there was a joke.

JERRY BURNS: When he'd be up in front of the team and he'd laugh, why every man in the room would laugh. And then he'd stop and they'd all stop. It was just

like that guy on "The Untouchables".

JOHN CRITTENDEN: He was laughing the last time I saw him, before the fourth Super Bowl in New Orleans at one of those week-of-the-game parties with buffet tables everywhere and Lionel Hampton's band playing. I had been cursed by Lombardi in losing dressing rooms and involved in staring matches with him when he didn't like my questions at press conferences, but I had never seen him laugh like this. He said, "You people write about me like I have horns and a pitchfork." He turned to the bar and said, "Get me another drink." And then he winked and said, "I didn't know they had parties like this at Super Bowl time!"

OCKIE KRUEGER: We were in a bar in Milwaukee having a drink and I guess we were talking pretty loud and raising our hands. So this fellow – the manager, the bouncer, whoever he was – comes up to Vince and says, "Coach, is this man bothering you?," and Vince got a twinkle in his eye and he said, "Yes, would you put him out of here?" There was quite a scene then and it ended up with Vince, who was in hysterics, pulling this guy off of me.

DUDS BILOTTI: It took me a little while to get to know him. There was a long funny period of hesitation. You see I didn't want to push myself on him. But it's funny how it happened. One night he and his group came in and the hostess comes to me and said that Mr. Lombardi wanted to see me. So I went over there wondering just what the hell he wanted and he grabbed me and said, "I got some people here I want you to say hello to." I admit it, I was shocked. I figured he was putting me on and I took a gamble and took a pinch of his cheek. I said, "Okay, baby, what have you got to say?" Everybody started to laugh and he laughed and from that time on it was good with us.

JACK TEELE: When he laughed, every bit of him laughed. He guffawed. I guess that is a comic strip word, but he really did.

MARIE LOMBARDI: He loved the writing of Art Buchwald. He used to carry around copies of Buchwald's books whenever we'd go out of town. One column he really loved was called, "How I Learned My Sex Life In The Corner Drugstore."

RAY BILOTTI: My son, who is 18 now, was working here bussing tables and one night there was a party and my son was bus boy on the party and he accidentally bumped into Mr. Lombardi as he was walking by with the tray. So my kid ad-libs, quick like, "Pretty

good block, huh?" I mean you never heard a man laugh like the way he did then. He was a real down-to-earth person.

DAD BRAISHER: The year we played the Cowboys in Dallas for the NFL championship we went to Tulsa to train during the week before the game, expecting their real good weather. We got down there and the weather in Tulsa was worse than it was in Green Bay and we had a terrible time. Of course Lombardi was upset. Before we had gone down there, I had asked him what he wanted in the line of equipment and he had told me. It didn't include anything heavy so when we were there and he needed it he'd say, "Hey, where's my heavy coat?," or "Where's my thermal underwear?," and I'd tell him he said he didn't want it and he'd say, "Next time see that I've got everything I need." So the next trip we made I put out a table in the dressing room just like a valet and I laid out everything you could possibly take. I even put some of those hall trees in there and hung up all the clothing you could take. Then I waited for him to come downstairs. I saw him go in there and I heard him laugh and say, "You crazy son of a gun you!"

DR. ANTHONY PISONE: He wanted to see an operation in the worst way so one day he stops by and I tell him to put on a scrub suit. We were working on a guy of 27 who'd had a knee shattered in a motorcycle accident. He was amazed at the way we pounded the pins in. He said, "I thought you doctors were gentle." Once that day I introduced Vince as "Dr. Lombardi" and a staff member asked him if he had a specialty. Without smiling, he said, "Backs."

LEW ANDERSON: A lot of his old Fordham cronies were at a party at his house in Washington. One old friend presented Vince with a large plaque reading, "Yea, though I walk through the valley of the shadow of death, I will fear no evil. For I am the meanest son of a bitch on the hill." He laughed until the tears rolled down his cheeks.

ZEKE BRATKOWSKI: One time we had a day off — I think it was the day after Thanksgiving — and Coach Lombardi was going to go deer hunting. So Bart and I got a white T-shirt and we painted a great big bullseye on it and put it on the bulletin board with a sign over it that said, "Italian Hunting Shirt." There were a lot of people who said, boy, you better not do that. They didn't know what his reaction would be. When he saw it he didn't know who had done it but when it got back to him that Bart and I had done it he kind of laughed.

DR. ANTHONY PISONE: Some organization in Green Bay voted him its Italian of the Year award in 1961. He said, "So where does that leave Pope John?"

PETE ROZELLE: Just after the merger in 1966, we had a meeting with all the old NFL owners at the Plaza Hotel. Emotions were still high and the situation was very tense. George Halas was upset over something else. The Rams had taken George Allen away from him and it was gnawing at him. He told me he wanted to bring up the subject of tampering with assistant coaches at this meeting but I said, "George, this isn't the place." I didn't want to create any ill feelings among the owners. Well, at the meeting George stood up and he said something like, "I think you know what's on my mind," and I thought, oh, no. George turned to Dan Reeves and he said, "What Dan Reeves did to me has been settled between us. We've made our peace. But as for George Allen – George Allen is a liar! George Allen is a cheat! George Allen is full of chicanery!" With each of these one-word blasts the temperature in the room dropped 10 degrees. At that moment Lombardi turned to Dan Reeves and said, "Dan, I think you've got yourself a winning coach." That just broke the whole room up – including George Halas. The meeting ended with everyone happy.

OCKIE KRUEGER: His laugh you could hear from one end of the country to the other. One night Phil Ford and Mimi Hines – this was in about 1961 – were at this place in Milwaukee which is now burned down and someone said, "This is a very funny couple," and so we had to go. Well, you know most entertainers, their act is 30 or 40 minutes but that night Phil Ford and Mimi Hines were on about four hours. She'd come over in that little mousey way and sit on his knee and he'd get in hysterics. It's the only time I've ever seen a man laugh so hard where the tears would just shoot out, shoot out about a foot!

MEL DURSLAG: In the midst of an interview one day he rose unaccountably. "That's it," he snapped and he walked away. I felt humiliated. "You're a dreamboat," I shouted after him. A short time later, in a Miami Beach restaurant, a waiter brought a bottle of wine to our table. "From the gentleman in the corner," he announced. And there was Vince, glass raised. "From dreamboat!," he said and he laughed uproariously.

DICK BOURGUIGNON: When he lost his first game – I'll never forget that one – when Tony Canadeo and

I walked in that Sunday night he was all alone and he said, "I had people here when we won. But after losing today I didn't expect anybody to come here. Except maybe you two guys." So we proceeded to tip a few. And it got to be about midnight and Marie came away from the girls in the other room – our wives were there, too – and she wanted to know what all the ruckus was because we were laughing and horsing around. And she stood there and said, "My God, I never thought I would see the day. You make it sound like we won today." And she said, "You know, in New York when they lost I couldn't talk to him until Wednesday or Thursday. That's when he first became a little bit human when he had lost a game." She said, "Here it is midnight and you've got the guy feeling as though he'd won the game."

MIKE MANUCHE: He told me he always put in a play that was a rinky-dink play, a ridiculous play where he might have six receivers going with the fullback throwing the ball. The guys would get a kick out of that kind of thing. He'd try to get some humor in there to loosen 'em up.

CHUCK LANE: One night I was in the shower. I was waiting for a date to come up here from Milwaukee and I had just moved into the second story of this boat house. So I was showering, baking my body for about half an hour, and then I heard this bellowing from downstairs and I thought to myself, hey, that sounds like Lombardi. Because you just don't mistake that howl for anything else. And all of a sudden there's a banging on my door. So I leaped out of the shower and wrapped a towel around myself and I went to the door, dripping. And I'll be darned if it wasn't Mr. and Mrs. Lombardi – and he is soaking wet – and he said, "What in hell are you doing?" – you know, his typical line – and I said, "What do you think I'm doing. I'm taking a shower," and he said, "Well, your goddamn shower is leaking all over me." I'll be darned if it hadn't. The tiles had come loose in the shower and the water had gone through the wall to the ceiling of this party room below me that was owned by a friend of the Lombardis. All of a sudden the water lets go and it's right over his seat and – splash! – he gets it. So he said, "Taking a shower?! With who?" I laughed and so did he. God, Vince Lombardi standing there soaking wet!

JERRY GREEN: Joe Schmidt's first game as head coach of the Lions was against the Packers in Green Bay in 1967. Schmidt walked into the visiting locker room at Lambeau Field that day and Lombardi came over from his side to greet him. Lombardi said, "Joseph, how are you? Good to see you." They shook hands then and later that afternoon Schmidt was asked about the greeting. Schmidt had been a player in the NFL for 13 years and someone mentioned that the old coach and the new one seemed to have a deep friendship. Schmidt said, "That was the first time he ever talked to me."

GEORGE HALAS: When we met someplace – not on a football field – we always would embrace each other. That seems sort of unusual for a couple of grown men, doesn't it? But I felt like that with Vince and the feeling was mutual. Maybe it was a couple of supposedly gruff old guys seeking solace with each other.

OCKIE KRUEGER: When I was at West Point, Red Blaik got a letter one day from Gen. MacArthur and when Blaik finished reading it he looked at me and said, "He's coming to West Point and he wants to sit on the bench." He had this great look of awe on his face. I mention this only because one day in the spring before Vince became sick he got a letter from Blaik and he said to me one day, "I've invited Col. Blaik to camp and he's accepted. He's coming." The expression on his face was the same as it was on Blaik's 25 years earlier.

¶ There was a lot of similarity between Blaik and Lombardi. I would look out the window and see Vince walking across the field and he would be walking in the same way that Blaik walked, with his hands behind him and his head hanging down a little, thinking.

JIM LAWLOR: We're in this restaurant and they're bothering him like crazy for his autograph and so he gets up and goes to the men's room and when he comes back he's laughing hysterically and the tears were coming down his cheeks. He says, "Now I've seen it all. I went to the men's room and I was standing there at the urinal and I get a tap on the shoulder and this guy's standing there with a placemat and a pen asking me for my autograph. He said he didn't want to bother me while I was having lunch."

DUDS BILOTTI: He didn't like to be bothered with autographs while he was having dinner but one time there was this young boy, maybe nine or ten, and this young girl, maybe five or six, and they came up to him. He shook hands with the boy and gave the girl a kiss. He was real loud and he said, "I told my friends I was hoping you two would come up

George Halas

and ask for my autograph. I was really hoping you'd ask." He made a big deal out of it and when the two kids walked back their parents waved. Lombardi stood up and bowed.

JIM FINKS: We had dinner together, the Player Rep committee, at Le Pavillion in New York. While we were eating we heard there was this tremendous crowd of people building up outside. You know, the New York autograph types. Gregory Peck's in the restaurant and so we figured that they were there for him. Well, Gregory Peck ate and left, without being bothered but when we came outside Lombardi was pinned to the building. It was him they wanted and they wouldn't let him get away until he had satisfied them. No one asked the rest of us, Arthur Modell, Well Mara, Muggsy Halas, Rankin Smith or me.

ARTHUR MODELL: A charwoman on the street in Chicago rushed up to him and asked him for his autograph. She probably'd never seen a game in her life.

EDWARD BENNETT WILLIAMS: Paul Brown could walk down Fifth Avenue at noon and nobody would recognize him. And he's a great coach. But Vince Lombardi! You couldn't walk on the streets of New York with him – and I did this many times – without having all the cops saying, "Hey, Vince," and the kids and the people calling out, "Hey, Vince." And he loved it, you know. He'd wave at them and shake hands and sign autographs. He loved it.

ED BRESLIN: He and New York, it was something! Like once we came out of Amalfi's at 6 o'clock and he decides he wants to go see his folks in Sheepshead Bay and I say to him, "You're crazy. You'll never get a cab to go out there." I wondered if we'd get a cab, period, because at 6 o'clock in Manhattan it's murder. But he waves his hand and this cab stops right there and this cabbie says, "Vince Lombardi!," like he's known him forever. And Vince says, "You won't like this but I'd like to go to Sheepshead Bay," and the cabbie says it doesn't matter, that he'd take him anywhere. Not only does this guy take Vince all the way out there but when he gets there he won't take a dime. He says it's been *his* pleasure.

BUD LEVITAS: Before a Pro Bowl in Los Angeles, we were in Le Bistro, the four of us, and Zsa Zsa Gabor was sitting at the table next to us. He was beaming and stretching his neck to get a better look at her. Everybody else in the place was looking at him.

MARIE LOMBARDI: He was oblivious to the notoriety,

really. I'd love to walk 10 feet behind him when we'd be walking down a corridor at O'Hare to catch a plane. Those open telephones they have, with 7 or 10 in a row. Every head would snap as he walked past and I almost could hear people say in unison on the phone, "You'll never guess who just went by here."

¶ We were in a restaurant and Maurice Chevalier was there, too. I didn't see Chevalier asked for one autograph. They just bothered Vince.

BUD LEVITAS: He was crazy about ice cream, just crazy about it. Just after he took the job with the Redskins he came to Palm Springs with Edward Bennett Williams to relax for a few days and the first thing he said when he landed – it was about 9 or 10 o'clock at night – was, "I gotta get some of that ice cream at Wil Wright's before it closes." So we drive like crazy from the airport but when we got to Wright's it was closed. There were only two guys there cleaning up and Vince says, "Damn." So Mr. Williams jumps out of the car and knocks on the window and five minutes later he's coming out with the biggest cones you ever saw. Vinnie was delighted.

RAY BILOTTI: I'd call him Mr. Lombardi if he was in one of those funny moods. If he was in a better mood I'd call him Vince. So he left you in a position where you did not know what to call him and if you got the grunt out of him he just nodded his head and you knew to leave him alone. Or if he'd smile and put out his hand and call you Ray then you knew fine, no problem. But then we wouldn't push him and he wouldn't care where he sat even. In fact there were times when he'd want to sit in the middle of the dining room. And if the grunt came we gave him privacy. That was the way we figured it out.

BUD LEVITAS: I took a lot of bus rides with he and the team and his mood was always different. There were times when he demanded silence and got it. And there were times when he demanded happy spontaneity and got that, too, of course. Like once all the guys in the back of the bus were singing and he leaned his head back and closed his eyes and said, "The boys are singing today and it sure sounds good."

OCKIE KRUEGER: People would say they couldn't wait to meet him and at luncheons and things they would come up to him and say, "Vince, I can't wait to talk with you," and pretty soon they'd go off. Later on I would go talk to these various people and I'd say, "Goodness, why didn't you stay and talk to him?, and they'd say, "Oh, I know so many people wanted to talk to him." Everyone thought so many people wanted to meet him but invariably it'd end up I'd be talking to him. I used to kid him about it. I'd tell him to change his deodorant and so forth and he really got sensitive about it.

LEAH LEVITAS: I never did believe the newspaper stories about him. He was a man who was sweet and gentle, almost mid-Victorian in his manner. He made a woman feel like a woman.

DUDS BILOTTI: There was a surprise party, and there were a lot of important people there. My brother and me, we will not be accused of being the best hosts in the State of Wisconsin and so when we walked in from the lounge us two dumb Italians didn't know where everybody was going to sit. Vince saw that there was a 10-second pause there and he started to tell everybody where to sit down. A surprise party for him and he was taking over! And you know he picked my wife, who barely knew him, to sit next to him. She was really petrified and she was holding my hand under the table. But before the night was over she was taking out pictures of our little girls and Vince was taking out pictures of his granddaughter and talking back and forth and laughing. She told me on the way home it was like she'd known him for 20 years. But that's the way he was. He may have been hard on football players and public relations men and the press, but he sure knew how to please the women.

MARIE LOMBARDI: He stopped cigarette smoking like that. He was very affected by the Surgeon General's report and another thing was he was getting a lot of letters from people, mainly kids, telling him how awful he looked on the sidelines puffing away.

STORMY BIDWILL: One time I went to St. Patrick's with him and Wellington Mara. Well told a joke about the devil who had a machine that got rid of people in an instant. He would throw 100 people in there and they would be gone in a second. Every once in a while he would put eight Italians in the machine. When asked why he said, "To grease the machine." Vince laughed and then came right back with an Irish joke.

ARTHUR MODELL: Once I told him, "You know my players on the Browns, they hold me in as close regard as the Notre Dame guys did Rockne," and he said, "Ah, crap." So I said, "Just the other day I heard two of them talking and one said, 'Let's win one for the gypper!' " Vinnie must have told a thousand people that one.

MARIE LOMBARDI: He was crazy about music – didn't know a lyric but he was crazy about music. And Sinatra! His special favorite. We went to a Sinatra show once in Miami and Frank insisted that we sit on stage. And the introduction he gave Vinnie! It was very special. Frank sang "My Kind of Town" that night but Vince said later that as far he he was concerned Frank could have substituted "New York" for "Chicago" in the song. He never stopped loving New York. Neither have I.

ETHEL KENNEDY: At the end of January 1970, Art Buchwald's play, "Sheep on the Runway," was opening in New York. Happily, the NFL held a conference in New York that afternoon and, at the last minute, Ed Williams and Vince joined a bunch of us who were going to the opening. Arriving with my in-laws, Jean and Steve Smith, the flashbulbs started popping. I saw Vince pale and he said, "Marie is not going to like this." It revised my thinking about the Coach. Maybe there *was* fear in him after all.

¶ In April, Kay and Rowland Evans, the Washington columnist, gave me a surprise birthday party. They knew the best possible present would be to have the Coach there. So they sat me at a tiny table with Vince, Rowland and Art Buchwald. It was a most happy seating arrangement. I was in heaven as the Coach went over the team player by player. Rowly and Art asked to be excused from the table sometime during the meat course, but we didn't hear them. After dinner I refused to go upstairs with the ladies as we still hadn't got to all the linebackers. Somewhere between the tight ends and the guards Marie came from my blind side to tell the Coach, "I want to see you in the locker room." Vince grinned and said, "See you soon."

¶ It was too soon. The next time we said goodbye was in St. Patrick's Cathedral.

Coach

**"They call it coaching, but it is teaching.
You do not just tell them it is so.
You show them the reasons why it is so
and then you repeat and repeat until they are convinced,
until they know."**

79

"This is a game for madmen. In football we're all mad. I have been called a tyrant, but I have also been called the coach of the simplest system in football, and I suppose there is some truth in both of those. The perfect name for the perfect coach would be Simple Simon Legree."

Coach: the seven-day work week

WILLIE DAVIS: When he said, "You were chosen to be a Packer," he made it sound like something unique and wonderful.

KEN IMAN: At the beginning of my rookie training camp we were watching films of one-on-one blocking by the rookies. Lombardi had been very critical and when the film came to me, he ran it back three or four times. He asked who he was watching and I said, "Iman." There was silence for a moment and I thought he was going to jump all over me. Instead, he said, "Good job, son." I felt that was the day I made the team.

COOPER ROLLOW: Once he roared at a rookie who obviously had no place in training camp, "You're not only big and fat but you're stupid, too." Later, he left the practice field to catch up with the rookie's homebound bus. He said, "I'm sorry, son. I had no right to embarrass you like that when you had no chance of making the team anyway."

PHIL BENGTSON: There was this kid from someplace in Louisiana and when he got to camp he was way overweight. Our opening routine in practice is that the players take three laps around the field to warm up and then they go to the coaches and start doing their own individual work until practice starts. But the first part of it was to circle the field three times until practice actually started. Well, this particular fellow, he got around the field one time – once! – before Vince told him to get out. "You're"– I forget exactly how he said it –"You're a physical disgrace." That was it. One lap and he was out!

JIM KENSIL: On the first of August, he'd tell me, "I'm gonna trade that guy," but when the season started whoever it was was always starting. Before the Packers played Dallas in the Salesmanship Game one year he said to me, "I'm going to get rid of that Gremminger," and if somebody'd been around right then to trade with I'm sure he would have traded him. But he'd sleep on something like that and his attitude would change. Gremminger not only started against Dallas but I think he played every game that year.

MARK DUNCAN: The first or second year I came to the commissioner's office I went out to Green Bay to give a rules talk. Lombardi liked to have meetings like that at the most difficult times and the most difficult of all in a training camp is right after the noon meal because you really have to fight to stay awake. So we were having the meeting then and things are going along pretty well and I happened to notice this one player. His eyes would drop and his head would drop and he'd wake himself up. I noticed that Lombardi was watching him. And sooner or later his head dropped and it never came back up and Lombardi walked over to him and he picked up the guy's playbook and he said, "Any man who can't stay awake in one of the most important meetings we have – the rules meeting, where you can learn something – why he doesn't belong in the Packers." And he told this guy to get out of the room, to get dressed and go home. He cut this guy right there. Maybe he was getting ready to cut this guy anyway. But he cut him right there.

¶ One year on one of our training camp visits I had developed a simple 20-question test which we gave to the players just before the meeting started to stimulate attention. I arrived in Green Bay with this test and he said, "What are we going to do today?," and I said, "Everybody is going to take a test," and he said, "Everybody?," and I said, "Everybody." So he called his assistants into his office and we passed out the test. It was an easy test but he had more fun taking it because he knew a couple more answers than his assistants. So now we got the squad together and passed the test out and he took great delight in walking around the room and looking at the answers that players were giving. He made a big thing out of that. He turned a routine rules briefing into a significant meeting.

DICK BOURGUIGNON: My son, Pete, worked for the Packers during training camp – until it was time to go back to school. He worked with Dad Braisher. And

Vince used to say to me, "There's a helluva kid," because Vince would have asked me if he ever said anything about this or that and I told him, very honestly, "The kid would never bring anything home." And Vince used to say, "What a helluva kid to keep his mouth shut." He liked that. And when Pete got home from school one night and we were all there, Pete walked over to Vince and he said, "I want to thank you for giving me this opportunity to work for you. I'm going to be a better man because I spent five summers working for you."

CHUCK LANE: He'd grant an audience to the writers on Mondays after reviewing the films. They'd come in and interview him. Well, they didn't really interview him because he would tell them and they would ask him what he wanted to be asked. That's what it amounted to.

CHUCK JOHNSON: Milwaukee is, oh, about 115 miles from Green Bay so I had to do a lot of my work with him by telephone. I'd call him every Tuesday morning at 9 o'clock and it would burn the hell out of him. So he'd be irritated and I'd say, "Well, I can call you Monday night. Or Tuesday afternoon. Would you rather have me call you then." And he'd snap, "No. Now what do you want today?" And so he'd answer my questions with a sharp "yes" or "no" or "that's a stupid question." Whenever he did that I'd run his answers just like that. The next week he'd always open up and say a little more.

MARIE LOMBARDI: He never missed a practice. Never. There were times when he went to bed with a high temperature and woke up with a higher one and I'd tell the doctor, "There's no way you're gonna keep him off the practice field today," and the doctor would say, "I know."

PAT SUMMERALL: There'd be a room with 60 men who were tired and worked hard all day. And they had a lot of things to say to each other. Sometimes it was hard to get them quiet. But Lombardi could walk into the room and clear his throat and the room would be silent.

ZEKE BRATKOWSKI: When he talked nobody ever stood to the back or side of him. He moved so he could talk to everybody. In our dressing room, he would stand in the middle and everybody was in front of him. And he always talked with notes.

ARTHUR MODELL: I swear to God, he had an eight-inch index finger. I used to tell him he'd never be able

to coach a team in Alaska because he wouldn't be able to talk with his hands there.

OCKIE KRUEGER: I told him, "Vince, if they ever cut off your forefinger you'll have to give up coaching football."

LIONEL ALDRIDGE: You didn't know how the guy was going to react to anything. It kept you off balance. It kept your mind working. Even when you thought he was probably treating you poorly he was probably actually helping you because he kept your mind active. That can't hurt.

HERB ADDERLEY: I remember one year we shut out the 49ers 13-0 and on Tuesday morning we went in and he kicked the trash can and it hit Jerry Kramer's chair which was right next to me. It put a big dent in the chair and a little cut on Jerry's leg. This was after a 13-0 victory! He was upset because the offense had moved the ball for a total of about 400 yards and scored but 13 points. He was disturbed at the defense because we had let them move the ball on us too much. He was really serious. That was the year we won our third title in a row.

FORREST GREGG: You could have a bad day against just about anybody and catch hell for it. The guy could be the greatest football player in the world. But I promise you right now, if you didn't play well against him you heard from Vince. When you went in to look at the film on Tuesday, you sweated blood. You started Sunday night thinking maybe you had a pretty good game. You woke up Monday morning saying, man, did I miss that block on that sweep?, or, how close did that guy come to getting to the quarterback on that certain play? You started to worry about all these things. You knew that if you goofed you were going to catch hell for it. You worried yourself half to death. Everybody would come in Tuesday morning with a big scowl on their face and you'd come in and look around and see what the atmosphere was like in the dressing room. And you'd try to get a look at him. He would be in the coaches' office and if he was in there with what we called that death look on his face, then we knew we were in for it.

BOYD DOWLER: Those movie sessions on Tuesday! He'd run the same play over six, seven times and you'd say to yourself, I'm gonna make it. He's not gonna notice me. And then on the eighth time he'd say, "And as for you, Dowler . . ." You *never* escaped his eye.

JOE DONNELLY: The players were watching a film Lombardi was running and someone kicked over a pop bottle. Lombardi said, "Keep those bottles off the floor." Then his deep voice boomed, "I could tell you guys fifty times to keep them off the floor but you'd still put them down there." You should have seen the heads snapping around and looking for misplaced bottles. Jim Taylor, Hornung, all of them.

DAVE SLATTERY: He was tremendously emotional and he used to laugh about it. He said, one day, "You just wait until you see me emote!"

CHUCK LANE: It was like watching the greatest Shakespearean character you've ever seen. He'd come in in the mornings and he'd walk into the dressing room and he'd have one face on. The other coaches would be sitting out drinking coffee in the other room, discussing things. And you could just see him. It was like he was off-stage then and he'd work himself into the proper mood and, boy!, when he came out of that room he came on ready, ready to go, and he was just like some kind of great actor taking the stage. I tell you it came off as a totally sincere performance. And it was a helluva performance to listen to when he'd go out there and get his troops around him.

He laughed. He cried. He prayed. He motivated. I think he could motivate almost anybody to do almost anything. He communicated with human emotions.

HAWG HANNER: I actually thought he was a soft-hearted man. I did. Some of the things he had to force himself to do because he believed they would help us. One day, in maybe my first or second year of coaching, everything had been going great for several weeks. We were having a good camp and he really hadn't gotten on anybody because everybody was in pretty decent shape. He came in one day and said that things just were going too smooth. He said he had to shake up people a little. And he wanted to know how everyone was doing and he said, "How's everyone's weight?" Somebody said, "Yesterday I was three pounds overweight"—which isn't much. So he started with that and before he was finished he had chewed just about everyone in there out.

PHIL BENGTSON: There were times when he was dressing when he'd pull on socks and say, "I'm just going to give these guys complete hell today. No matter what happens. Because today is going to be one of those days." And it was effective. He said many times that the team was going to have a lousy practice unless we did something about it. So he would go after them with that in mind. And I pitied the first guy who stepped out of line because he was the guy who was going to get it. He had no qualms about going after anybody. It didn't matter who it was—Hornung or Starr or who. It didn't make any difference if it was an outstanding football player or how much experience he had or what position he played, he went after them.

JERRY BURNS: One day he took off after Willie Wood and Herb Adderley. It was in the pre-season and neither of them had signed yet and he was mad about it. You wouldn't have believed this tirade—15 minutes, at least, of shouting. And the room we were in—I forget where it was—was incredibly hot. When he was through he walked into the next room and I walked in there with him. He took out his handkerchief and wiped off his forehead. He was smiling. He said, "You know, I'm just getting too old for all of this."

¶ He was unhappy and he was pacing the locker room and dishing out holy hell and when he passed by this table full of footballs he reached down to pick one up. It was one the players had been autographing and he held it in his hands for a long time before he looked down—now understand he's really been shouting—and he said, "You guys don't deserve to have your names on a football! You don't deserve to be called Green Bay Packers!" And then he started yelling, "Dad! Dad!"—that's our equipment man, Dad Braisher—and when Dad ran into the room, all excited because he didn't know what was going on, Lombardi started throwing footballs at him, pelting him. He said, "Get these goddamn things out of here! It's a disgrace!"

ART DALEY: Vince had a great deal of pride in his guards, perhaps because he was a guard himself and they are so important in the protection of the quarterback and in opening up holes. Walking off the practice field once he fumed, "I'm tired of making chicken salad out of chicken shit." He was talking about his guards. Another time—a couple days after as a matter of a fact—he boomed, "We got the best damned offensive line in the league. Just you wait and see."

HENRY JORDAN: One time at a meeting he got on our guards something awful. It was so bad everybody came out of the meeting objecting. We were saying to each other, "He's got no right to talk to any of us like that." I can remember there was a group of us talking and just then we passed a room. We looked in and there were the guards and they had their playbooks open and they were studying. Then it dawned on me that Lombardi was right. He had a message to give and he got it across.

FUZZY THURSTON: Having been a guard himself, I think he expected just a little bit more out of Kramer and myself. We were the keys to the offense.

TOM BROWN: He would holler at you and harrass you so much that you would say to yourself: You'd better not blow it or it's all over for you. He instilled that in you and I can't explain why. I've tried lots of times, at banquets and things, but you really had to have been there and played for him.

SAM HUFF: Once he cut a player at a meeting. This guy came in late – actually he was 10 minutes early but that meant he was late – and Vince said, "You! You're holding everybody up here!" And the guy says that he was waiting to see the doctor about his leg but that the doctor didn't show up. The guy said, "The doctor was gone when I got there but I waited to see if he'd come back." And Vince – he's steaming – said, "Mister, you report to the Roanoke Buckskins tomorrow!" You could have heard a feather drop.

ART DALEY: There were four games in which the offense went to hell and on the Thursday after the 6-3 game with the Rams, Vince got furious in practice with the offense and it was the first time I ever saw him slap a player, one of his offensive tackles, as we prepared for the Vikings. He dressed down all of the offensive players and I finally left with the air blue. Two days later Vince was laughing it up at the 5 o'clock club the night before the game in Minneapolis and I mentioned the fire of Thursday to him. He chuckled and said, "We'll see if it does any good tomorrow." The Packers won the game 38-13.

DAVE SLATTERY: He'd come in and laugh at himself and say, "Oh, I was mean today." He got off a great line one time. He said, "I hate people to use bad language but goddammit, I'm awful during the football season."

CHUCK LANE: Sometimes he would come out of a team meeting and he'd go into the coaches' room and close the door. I talked to people who knew him and they said he'd go in there and throw up and almost have a seizure. This was in his last year as coach here, 1967.

EDWARD BENNETT WILLIAMS: After he would have a horrendous scene with some player in which he would just lace him, he would be emotionally debilitated. He would be exhausted and he'd feel terrible about having done it. He wouldn't have regretted that he'd done it. He just would feel terrible that he had to do it.

JIM LAWLOR: So I said to him, "What are you so hard for?," and he said, "I was hired here to produce winning football teams and that's what I'm going to produce. I don't hold any malice about them sneaking out but I can't afford to let one go because then the rest of them are going to go."

DOM GENTILE: A first-year man, Joe Scarpati, was cut from the squad and he came down to the practice field and pleaded with Vince to stay. Scarpati was crying. He told Vince that it was a dream of his to play for the greatest coach in the world. We were loaded with defensive backs and Vince told him that he was sure he could get him with another team. I happened to be standing near them at the time and when Joe left, coach walked over to me and he had tears streaming down his cheeks. He said, "It's guys like that who make this all worth it." Joe went on to play for the Eagles and the Saints.

WELLINGTON MARA: It was after practice one day and he was in a hurry to get out of the parking lot. He really *could* shower and dress in seconds. Just by coincidence Marie had parked behind him and when he came out she was talking to a group of people. He said, "Get this thing out of here," but she didn't move as fast as he wanted her to. When she did get in the car she backed it out about six feet before it stalled. Meanwhile he was flooring his car and, well, you can imagine what happened. He was just beside himself and he jumped out of his car and shouted, "Why don't you learn how to drive?" And she shouted back, "Why don't you shut up!" That broke him up.

BILL FORESTER: You couldn't believe how much he wanted to win the games that didn't count – those after we had clinched our division title.

BOYD DOWLER: It was after – and before – a game with someone like Pittsburgh that he really was on us. It was like he'd decide that a Wednesday practice was going to be a lousy practice and it would be. And then he'd decide a Thursday practice would be a good one and it was. He threw all of himself into everything we did and all he asked was the same from us.

JOHN SYMANK: There were rules and standards and if they weren't followed then someone caught it. I remember he told the manager of a big hotel on the

"I've never known a man worth his salt who in the long run, deep down in his heart, didn't appreciate the grind, the discipline. There is something in good men that really yearns for discipline."

West Coast that he would pull the team out unless the food service got better. The next meal we had four additional waitresses. And I'll never forget the time he destroyed the film of a San Francisco photographer for taking pictures in a closed practice session. Another time the president of the Packers, Mr. Olejniczak, came down on the field to talk to him. And coach blew up and he said, "You want to talk with me, you make an appointment with my secretary. Don't you ever bother me on the practice field again."

HOWARD COSELL: I responded to him because he was just dead honest. We'd make a deal and that was it. Oh, he was so quick, so impatient, so desirous to get things done that he would say things without realizing what he was saying. When I went out to shoot "Run to Daylight" in 1964, Vince and I made a deal and he allocated such and such hours to me each day. Now the first day I'm out on the practice field and Vince is going beserk out there. He suddenly screams at me, "Goddamit, you're all the same! Give you guys an inch and you take a mile! Get the hell off this field and stay off it." I told my director to tell the crew to pack up. I didn't have to take that shit. I made a deal and it's not going to work and I'm leaving. So I left. Back at the hotel later I got a call. He said he wanted to do the show and do it just as we had agreed. I realized then that he had absolutely no malice. None. That he had simply shouted in the heat of impatience and excitement. I told the crew to go back to the damn field and he was just great. We were the only people he ever let in the locker room to shoot his speech.

JOHN PROSKI: He didn't like the shape the field was in and he chewed me in front of the whole team. Chewed me good. This Tex Maule from *Sports Illustrated,* he's there and he puts it in his story. So the next Monday or so Lombardi says to me – he's trying to make up now – he says, "I see you got your name in *Sports Illustrated,*" and me, I said, "No thanks to you."

LARRY BROWN: He never treated me like a rookie. After he knew who I was and after he'd been watching me awhile – when he began paying any attention at all – he treated me like a veteran. I was just out of college and he was on me like I was a third-year pro, yelling at me the way I suppose he yelled at Paul Hornung and Jim Taylor. Once he chewed me out so unfairly – I thought so, anyway – that I began to hurt inside. I was hurting with hate for this man. Three or four days later he came up to me again –

just as unexpectedly and for no better reason that I could see — and he put his hand on my back and said, "Good play. You're going to be a good boy."

JOE BLAIR: He made you feel like a million bucks right after you felt like two cents a minute before.

COOPER ROLLOW: An offensive end slipped and fell when he was hit running a post pattern in practice. The end didn't get up and a Packer trainer raced onto the field with a medical kit. "Get away from him," Lombardi bellowed. "Leave him alone! He either stands up on his own and becomes a Green Bay Packer or he crawls off the field and out of the league." The stricken player rose groggily, rejoined the huddle and went on to become an All-Pro.

JOE BLAIR: He would be walking one way with his back to the group and all of a sudden he would turn around and scream and yell at someone, saying, "What in hell are you doing, mister?!" The ground would tremble.

BOB SKORONSKI: The game plans were completely designed by Vince — on both the passing and running games. I can't say every single game, but the great majority of them.

FORREST GREGG: We would start off early in the week with a game plan and then he would pick it apart from there.

JERRY BURNS: It was amazing, that's the only way to describe it. He would study the film, then go to an owners' committee meeting at 11 o'clock and talk there for two hours and then come back to us at 1 and tell us exactly how it was going to be in the next game. His mind never stopped.

PHIL BENGTSON: I had complete authority of the defense — as complete as you can have — but he was still the head coach. He would come in and discuss football with us, the defense, but not very often and seldom when we didn't ask him to. Oh, once in awhile just to pass the time of day he would. He'd hear that projector going and he'd wonder what we were going to do with this and that.

WILLIE DAVIS: When we were getting ready for a game it was like he could see in his mind what was going to happen. He would stand up there in front of us and he'd say, "I can see Paul with that ball cutting through that seven hole." Or, "And Willie coming through there, knocking those guys on their asses and coming down on that quarterback."

TEX MAULE: The changes he would make were subtle ones, like changing blocking assignments, switching keys. He was a great believer in optional pass blocking. He wanted his players to read the defense, zone or man-to-man, after coming off the line. He wanted them to switch their tactics in that moment. It's things like that that set him apart.

LARRY BROWN: He meant a little more than most people realized by this thing he called running to daylight. He meant doing it in one continuous motion. If the hole is plugged you don't stop to look for another one. You keep running — keep accelerating — as you look. He hated dancing. He despised fancy dans.

PAT PEPPLER: I always felt Lombardi was under-rated as a football mind. I think he had a brilliant football mind. The fact that his offense was simple didn't mean that it wasn't well thought out and that he didn't know a lot of complicated things or was incapable of complicated things. It was simple because he thought this was the best way to operate. His offense actually was a lot subtler than people thought.

¶ Here's what he did: The other team's defense would be giving him some trouble. So if you want to make two or three changes from a simple game plan which is almost automatic in people's minds, then you'd go in at halftime — and particularly with a veteran club — and you'd say, all right, we're gonna do this. Instead of blocking this way we'll block that way. And so his teams always adjusted easily. It got to be like brushing their teeth and combing their hair.

PHIL BENGTSON: A lot of his reputation came from his psychological handling of the players and so a lot of people have tended to ignore his football mind. He had no question about how to do this or how to do that in football. He had spent his whole life preparing.

¶ The so-called Green Bay sweep was from his own imagination. Nobody else had used that play at the time and everybody does now.

HAWG HANNER: He would never second-guess any player. Of course he never did give you any options. There was only one way and that was Lombardi's way.

BART STARR: I worked with him so long that I knew what he wanted. He made it explicitly clear what he wanted. He didn't leave anything to chance. He didn't leave any hesitation on your part. He just laid it out in black and white: "If they do this, then I want you to do that." It was just that clear cut. And if you did that, even if you erred, if you did what he said he wanted, he would never be on you. And if you didn't

"Not only must I show them how, I must also show them why. Once they understand a play they can do it."

adhere to what you said, if you started to free lance, then he would be on your back. Because he wanted it done a certain way. *His* way.

JIM RINGO: He never felt that a football player should have to think on the field. He felt they have too many other things to think about. So our system was very simple. We had a trap and the trap was just a trap, regardless of the number of people the other team'd put up there. What he was concerned with was the execution of that trap. And when we ran a pass play we ran that pass play to execute that play against a particular defense. Now if they changed that defense, naturally he taught the men to be able to change their patterns to fit what the defenses were throwing at us. He expected a lot of people to think on the field to the degree that it would come automatically.

¶ He never would take a man and expect him to do something he knew he couldn't do. He would want the most that man could do in his particular skill but he would never take him beyond that. He would never expect Paul Hornung to run 100 yards for a touchdown because he knew Paul didn't have the speed. The same with Jimmy Taylor. But you would expect something out of Max McGee. When he caught one you would expect him to go all the way, because he had the speed. You wouldn't expect Fuzzy Thurston to be very good on one-on-ones. But he could pull, so you realized that he was a pulling guard. Even I couldn't do one-on-ones sometimes. I would get a big man over top of me and that was it. So why use it? Vince *didn't*, either.

WILLIE DAVIS: He liked to make you responsible for things, to establish responsibility on the field. I think this is why he left things so simple. He didn't want to create doubts in players' minds. He wanted to have a situation where he could hold you responsible for what you did or didn't do. That was it on Tuesdays. I mean, he would accept a certain amount of physical inability to do something – like being blocked now and then. But the cardinal sin was to remain blocked – to be out-thought. There were times when he'd assume things, assume that you knew what you should do without being told. We were getting ready to play the Giants once, working on a contain defense against Tarkenton. In practice we called a blitz but the linebacker on my side didn't go so I went in. I think it was Zeke Bratkowski who was the quarterback then, he scrambled and got outside. Vince was all over me. I was so surprised and shocked

that I snapped back at him. I said, "What was I supposed to do?," and he said, "Mister, is it too much to ask you to use your head?"

FUZZY THURSTON: I played for three coaches before I came here. George Halas, Weeb Ewbank and Buck Shaw. In pure knowledge of football, their level was basically the same as Lombardi's. The difference was that Lombardi got production and he got it by selling himself to us and us to ourselves. He got more out of his players. That was what put him a cut above everyone else.

BOB SCHNELKER: He did it with words. He could get up in front of that group of 40 players and five or six assistant coaches and he would get up and say what they wanted to hear. He always knew the exact time, too. He could get up there in front of the group and I don't care whether it was on Tuesday or on Wednesday or on the Saturday night before the game, he always knew exactly when to do it and exactly what to say. There's such a fine line between winning and losing and I think the fact that he could do this – this molding of emotions – that this was the thing that made him successful. He had all the words and that great voice, but most of all he had the timing. He had the knack of getting 40 players to the point where they just couldn't wait to get out there on the field and play.

DOMINIC OLEJNICZAK: He told me about one player. He said, "Coach"– he called me coach –"I just got rid of a helluva good football player." And I said, "You did? Why would you do that?," and he said, "Well, I'll tell you. I don't want any bad apples in my organization. I get one apple in the bushel over here and the rest of them will start rotting, too." The player he got rid of was one great player. An All-Pro.

JERRY BURNS: He said, "In pro football the balance of personnel is so even that the difference between success and failure is player control – in every phase."

DOM GENTILE: One morning we were standing around the airport waiting to enplane and Vince and Jerry Kramer were discussing the reserve clause in player contracts. It was being tested and there was the possibility that it might go. Lombardi said, "Jerry, if this goes, it will be the end of pro football."

ZEKE BRATKOWSKI: Really, he was a great salesman with a football mind. He could come up with new ways of attacking zones, man-to-man coverage, that type of thing. But his enthusiasm and salesmanship, these things were really what taught us. He was just bubbling over when he'd talk to us. And then we'd go out on a field and he demanded execution. Like completing 50% of your passes in practice, that was just a mediocre performance. I mean he demanded that everything be caught. There was no excuse for the ground being muddy, slippery or wet. You had to stand up and do what was demanded of you. If it was windy, he wouldn't accept the wind as an excuse or if the ground were frozen you just weren't allowed to slip. You'd have to adjust. He never said, "That would have been a good pass except the wind was bad." Never.

SAM HUFF: Pat Richter went to block the defensive man out in a nutcracker drill. He blocked the linebacker out all right but he also caught a forearm across the face. Wow! His nose was flattened and there was blood gushing all over! Now you've got to understand that Richter's a big man, 6-5 or so. So Lombardi, who must have been nearly a foot shorter, rushes over and picks Richter up off the ground and shakes him. And Lombardi says, "If you'd put your face in there right you wouldn't get your nose pushed in!"

FORREST GREGG: He didn't believe in shoulder blocks. He believed all blocking should be done with the head. Because he felt if you hit the guy in the center – you aim for the center of the guy – and if he made a move to the left or to the right you are going to catch him with something at least. He said you stick your head where the guy bends and then you keep your feet moving and drive him.

FUZZY THURSTON: He'd say, "Put your nose right in the other guy's numbers. The neck bone is the strongest bone in the body. You can't possibly hurt the neck bone."

BART STARR: He was a great slogan man. A lot of people would find putting slogans on the wall almost intolerable. They couldn't stomach it. Yet he had a way of doing it that you not only didn't resent it you kind of looked forward to it and enjoyed it.

GEORGE HALAS: You might reduce Lombardi's coaching philosophy to a single sentence: In any game, you do the things you do best and you do them over and over and over.

WELLINGTON MARA: His theory of learning was repetition. He'd say, "You gotta seal off the linebacker! You gotta seal off the linebacker! You gotta seal off the linebacker!" He etched it on their minds.

"The harder you work the harder it is to surrender."

"Some of us will do our jobs well and some will not, but we will all be judged by only one thing—the result."

"Fatigue makes cowards of us all."

"Mental toughness is essential to success."

"Make that second effort."

"Success demands singleness of purpose."

"Winning is not everything. It is the only thing."

"If a man is running down the street with everything you own you won't let him get away. That's tackling."

ZEKE BRATKOWSKI: So we'd look at the movies, Bart and I, and we'd take notes and maybe we'd repeat the same note 10 times. And then we'd underline it.

FRANK WALL: In Hawaii he said, "Frank, there's something wrong with my damn swing and I'm going to find out what." He was on the practice tee then. I left and when I came back two hours later he was still there. His shirt was soaked with sweat and there were golf clubs strung out all over the ground. He said, "Watch this. I've got it!" And he hit a perfect shot.

JOHN SYMANK: Coach was very methodical in his approach – almost to the extent that it was boring. However, we knew what to do, when to do it and *why* we did it.

VINCE LOMBARDI, JR.: I don't think if anyone told him he was wrong he'd agree with them. He'd say, "You're nuts." But by the end of the day he'd say, "You know, you might have something there."

TOM FEARS: If you suggested anything to the coach you would confront a negative attitude almost 100% of the time. "No," would come out right away. But he was a smart man. He'd think about the idea and if it was any good then the next day he'd change it a little and introduce it. He was a hard man to argue with but it was easy to plant something with him. You couldn't say, "Vince, I've been checking their tendencies and I think we can do so-and-so." That would get a fast reject. But you could say, "Coach, it looks like they are doing something like we saw a couple of weeks ago and at that time you said maybe such-and-such would work." Maybe he never said anything like that at all but if you did it that way he'd listen to you.

JIM TAYLOR: We were so attentive to what he had to say because everything that he mentioned was so very important we had to take it with a lot of seriousness. I think afterwards some of it soaked in. Or you thought about it after you left the meeting room – the pep talks and the things he mentioned. I know lots of times different players would bring them up again later.

FORREST GREGG: His idea of the offense was that it reflected the personality of the coach. And he liked the idea of all the coordination of a vast number of human beings to make a running game work – the interdependence of the players. Coordination. That's the thing he talked about, getting us all to think alike and getting us all to react alike in certain situations.

JIM TAYLOR: There wasn't any jealousy on the club, no envy of, say, one particular receiver making All-Pro and the other not making it. This kind of thing causes friction on other clubs. We had as much unity as you possibly could have, which goes along with the love aspect he always talked about.

¶ There were never one or two or five or seven plays in a ball game on which you had no assignment. Everyone had an assignment on *every* play. He was paying you well and he expected you to execute each individual play.

¶ He minimized the mistakes by working on only a certain number of plays for particular situations. So each time you saw a defense you knew that you should react like this and that everyone else would do the same. The timing would do it. And we didn't have 40 plays to run. We had 15 to 20.

ART DALEY: Coming back from a game I was reading Time magazine, a story on Robert McNamara, then secretary of defense, and McNamara said he never would be interviewed by just one member of the press. He always wanted at least two. I told this to Vince and he laughed. "That's the way I want it, too," he said. But he never really stuck with it. Once, though, I interviewed him in his office alone during the off-season with no particular story idea in mind. I remarked that if we talked long enough I'd hit on a story. He talked a minute more and then excused himself, presumably, I thought, to step into the men's room. He never returned and I finally left.

TEX MAULE: Whenever they'd get to a new city Vinnie would read off the list of bars and restaurants that were off-limits. Well, they'd get to Chicago on a Saturday and of course the list there was a long one. Once Lombardi read what must have been a list of 200 bars and when he got through he was furious, just because it had taken so much time to read them. So Max McGee says, "Jeez, coach, you don't expect me to make all of those places in one night, do you? Next year let's come down on a Friday at least." Vinnie damn near split a gut.

DON CHANDLER: I think everybody who played for him felt the pressure just a little bit more because you knew if you didn't do well – what he asked you to do – that you'd have to contend with him.

BOYD DOWLER: He never could accept anything less than a maximum effort – and that included practices, too. He would say, "If you can't take *my* pressure then for sure you can't take it in a game." He could rip you in those practices. I know there were many times when I was just as nervous — more sometimes — going to practice as playing in a game. And it worked. On third-and-10 in a close game, in a championship game, you really believed you could do it. It sounds unreal but that's the way it worked.

DAD BRAISHER: It was real quiet in the locker room — more quiet than normal — and he said, "How about a little music in here to pep things up?"

PHIL BENGTSON: We went out to play the 49ers in '68 and we had all these guys hurt. The guys were noticeably worried, noticeably tense. It reminded me of several times when our good teams were the same way — just tense as hell. Five minutes before we were to go out on the field Vince would tell a joke, a story about something he thought was funny, to try to get them to laugh.

MAX MC GEE: His speeches were fantastic, although they got a little old after you'd been there for awhile. I always figured he was preaching to the people who get the hell beat out of them all the time — the guards, the tackles, the defensive people. Flankers take their licks, but I wasn't out there getting hit every play. Me, I played the same with or without emotion. I liked the speeches and sometimes I've seen the whole team turn around and run through the door — that's how high he got them. But most of the time when he was talking I was half asleep.

DICK BOURGUIGNON: I've read all the stories about Rockne and how great he was. Well, I was in the Packer locker room many times and I thought, everything I've read about Rockne and what I'm hearing here today, Rockne couldn't hold a candle to Vince Lombardi.

BOB SKORONSKI: He presented one game as a challenge to players. He said, "Nobody here wants to win." A couple of guys got up in the middle of the speech and said, "I want to win," and then another guy got up and said, "I want to win, too, coach." He wanted this to happen. I'm sure he planned it. He was just checking a few guys out and he wanted some guys to get up and burst out that way. He wanted us to say, "Wait a minute, coach, you are wrong. I'm here to win."

HENRY JORDAN: He pushed you to the end of your endurance and then beyond it. And if there was a reserve there, well, he found that, too.

WILLIE DAVIS: Before the big games, there were certain guys he knew he had to communicate with. He'd call me

in and tell me that the key was us guys up front. He'd make me feel confident. Like he'd say, "There is nobody who can stop you from getting that quarterback if you want to." I'd believe him. It worked during a game, too. We'd come off the field after a series and he'd say, "We're just not getting to that quarterback. Make up your mind, Willie, I've seen you do it." And I'd go back out there and maybe on the second or third effort I'd get through. It was like we'd done it together, coach and I.

BOB SKORONSKI: He could romance a block, even on the toughest guy, to the point where the guy who was going to do it really thought he enjoyed this thing.

BOYD DOWLER: His big word was "horseshit". When he'd get mad he'd steam and his face would get colored and he'd say, "Mister, that was *horseshit.*" Oh, that word, he knew how to use it. He would call me Boyd when I'd done something well, Dowler when I'd done something fairly well and when I'd do something badly , well . . . he'd use my full name. He'd say, "Boyd Dowler, that was *horseshit.*"

MAX MC GEE: Once I dropped a nothing pass in a game we were leading by something like 28-0. It hit me in the nose and I dropped it. Vince was beside himself. He wanted us to be playing our best every moment. He came over to me and he was hollering and letting me have it so I told him, "Coach, you could get any guy off the street to catch those kind. You pay me to catch the hard ones." That was the wrong thing to say. He screamed at me for another half hour.

VINCE LOMBARDI, JR.: I know for a fact that there were a few times on the sidelines when he'd get so mad that he'd literally pass out and need oxygen.

KEN IMAN: In my second year, when we were playing the Rams, Jerry Kramer busted a shoestring and I had to go in for one play. During the play I managed to make three blocks. Watching the films on Tuesday, Bill Austin brought the play to the attention of Lombardi – as if he needed to. Lombardi walked over to me, patted me on the head and said, "That's a good boy."

¶ That same year, Bart called an audible and thinking of the play I missed the snap count and messed up the play. It was only a practice but Lombardi yelled, "You stupid son of a bitch! How do you expect to play in this league if you can't remember the snap count?" I haven't made a late snap since then.

BART STARR: He'd say, "Listen, I know you can't be perfect. No one is perfect. But boys, making the effort to be perfect, trying as hard as you can, is what life is all about." And then he'd say, "Boys, if you'll not settle for anything less than the best, you will be amazed at what you can do with your lives. You'll be amazed at how much you can rise in the world." I think this consistent unwillingness to settle for anything less than excellence was the greatest thing he left with people around him.

TOM LANDRY: It was the suffering together that made the Packers a great team. And Vince made them suffer.

¶ It takes a special kind of character to know when to let up, when to back off. He would get them to the point when they were just about ready to do anything and then he was able to crack a joke or he was able to do something to break the tension and put them back on the right track.

CHUCK JOHNSON: When Jerry Kramer was deadly sick that time – the time they found the splinters in his groin – there was a lot of talk that maybe Jerry had cancer or something like that. So I went to Vince and said I was going to have the Journal's medical writer, a fellow named Jim Spaulding, call the Packer team physician. Vince exploded. "Have him call me," he said. "I'll tell him what's wrong. Me! I'll give him all the answers." I went to Spaulding and I told

him to call the doctor, and a story ran that Sunday on what the doctor thought. The story was the first full picture of what Kramer's ailment was all about. Well, that day the Packers lost to Minnesota and when I came down to the locker room Lombardi was coming out. Now usually he was best in his dealings with the press after a loss but this day he jumped on me – right in front of a lot of people – and said, "What do you think you're doing? What right do you have to print Kramer's physical condition without asking me? What kind of friend are you?"

SAM HUFF: I was hurt one time and I was limping and feeling pretty lousy in a workout one day. But I wasn't loafing. I was giving it everything I've got. And we're out there running and hitting the sleds and he yells out, "Hey! Hey, you! Number 70! Let's run! Let's move it!" Honest to God, he didn't know it was me.

JIM TAYLOR: He would come into the training room and say, "Nobody's hurt here," and everybody would get up off the tables and walk out. They got better right away.

DOM GENTILE: He never believed in injuries. It wasn't a part of his nature to even think about injuries. And he so completely sold himself to the players that they just believed everything he said, regardless if they were injured. They absolutely believed everything he said. If he said they could go out and play they would at least go out and try to play. He didn't want you to play if you were hurt. Now when I say hurt, I mean *hurt* – not a sprained wrist or a turned ankle or something like that. He expected you to play then.

PAUL HORNUNG: Once I had some really bad strained ligaments and Lombardi said to me, "You can't hurt them more. You might as well play." So I did.

JIM RINGO: I was laid up in the hospital with boils. It was very painful and I didn't think there was a chance I could play. I figured there was no sense even making the trip to Cleveland but he said that I was a member of the team and I had to be there. So I went. To watch. Before the game he talked to me about how each man fit into the overall picture of being a champion. He talked about the easy way out. They shot Novocain into my boils and I played that day.

KEN IMAN: He told us, "The Good Lord gave you a body that can stand most anything. It's your mind you have to convince."

BUD LEVITAS: The 5 o'clock club began at just that – 5 o'clock in Vinnie's suite – and it would last for one hour. At 10 seconds before 6 the room would empty.

MAL FLORENCE: During that hour he was charming and informative, although he made it clear that everything was off the record. Woe to the man who broke that confidence. Vince would have cut him out of the herd. And when he'd had enough chit-chat, he would simply say, "Gentlemen, I'm going to take a nap before dinner but you're welcome to stay here and drink if you choose." That was the end of the party.

BOYD DOWLER: God, how he hated excuses! Alibis of any kind. In 1960, on a pattern I broke 10 yards out on the right side. It was the sun field and I lost the ball totally. It fell, oh, maybe 10 yards away. In the films on Tuesday he asked what had happened on that play – knowing full well what had happened. And I said, "I was running blind and I didn't have time to adjust. The sun –" And he interrupted and said, "You're an NFL receiver, right? Well, mister, then it's your job to catch the ball."

MAX MC GEE: There were times when you'd hear guys say they hated him. But I don't think they really did. They hated the things he made them do. He was making them play better than they were capable of.

BOB SKORONSKI: Lionel Aldrige would be out there and Lionel would think that he had made a great play and then he would hear Lombardi yell, "Hey, what the hell are you doing?" And something would happen to him and the next time they would run the same play he would kill them.

HAWG HANNER: He didn't have a lot to do with the defense unless somebody wasn't hustling. He'd notice a guy wasn't moving on the ball and he'd ask the guy, "What defense were you in?"

BOYD DOWLER: The only time I ever talked back to him was during a game. He'd give me or maybe the whole team one of those verbal tirades from the sidelines, screaming with his hands at his side. I'd holler back at him. I'd tell him to go to hell or to shut his mouth. He didn't mind. I think he figured that we should be just as emotionally involved as him.

WILLIE DAVIS: One game – I don't remember which one but it's unimportant, it could have been any game – we hadn't played very well in the first half and he was beside himself at halftime. He told us, "You're a disgrace. If you quit on me you'll never live it down. The way you played it's obvious we didn't work

enough. We won't be guilty of that next week."
And the practice the previous week had been hell.
He made us fear him, I know that. We went out
and won that game, won it big.

ZEKE BRATKOWSKI: I can remember when we won six games in a row and then got beat by somebody. We came into that locker room quiet. There was no laughter because he had a thing on the wall: "There is no laughter in losing." And everybody had a kind of hound dog expression on their face. They didn't know what he was going to say. So he got up there in front of everybody and he chewed us out for our hound dog looks! He said, "Who do you think you are that you didn't think you could get beat? What makes you think that you are that good that you can't get beat." He took the direct opposite approach to what we had figured.

BOB SKORONSKI: Once we lost a game and he stood in the locker room – it was almost comical – in Green Bay and said, "You guys don't want to win. You don't deserve this carpeting."

¶ We played the Cardinals in Jacksonville and we beat them 41-14 and when the game was over I can remember walking off the field and I was walking casually and some guy yelled, "Hey, you'd better get in here!" Lombardi was standing on a chair in the middle of the room screaming. And I thought, God, I must be in the wrong locker room. I thought we won.

MARIE LOMBARDI: We played the Cardinals and we won. Big. 41-14. But it was a sloppy game. It was over about 11 o'clock and I was sitting in the bus waiting. The locker room must have been a block away and I know it was closed up. I heard yelling and fussing, though, and I knew it was him. I heard him use the word midnight over and over. They came out in the bus after that and when he came out and sat beside me I said, "Did you eat the kids out?," and he said, "Yeah, what about it?" Once he got mad he didn't know where to stop. I asked him about the curfew and he said it was for midnight and I said that was unreasonable. "My God," I said. "Give them a break. They did win." So he stood up and announced that curfew was being pushed back to 1 a.m. When the players were filing off the bus – he got off first alone – every one of them stopped by and said something. I told Paul, "Do you want me to talk with him again? I'll get it pushed back to 2 o'clock."

CARROLL DALE: I paid close attention to what he said when we won a game. That was when Lombardi was most critical. After a loss he seemed to be trying to keep our confidence up. When we won he criticized in detail. He seldom got on you for physical errors, though. When you played regularly for Lombardi as a receiver, he assumed you'd catch most balls and drop some. I'll never forget one day he shouted at me. It was in practice in 1965. I had been running a turn-in pattern but Willie Davis had put the pressure on Bart and the ball wasn't there when I hooked around. So naturally I just eased up. How could I get a ball that hadn't been passed? Coach ignored the man who missed the block and came storming up to me. "Carroll," he yelled, "that's the last time I ever want to see you stand away from the ball. If it isn't there start moving back to the quarterback and keep moving until you get there. You're the guys who cause interceptions – receivers just standing around."

BOB SKORONSKI: Vince would say, "You know you never win a game unless you beat the guy in front of you. The score on the board doesn't mean a thing. That's for the fans. You've got to win the war with the man in front of you. You've got to get your man."

PETE ROZELLE: He was a highly ethical person. He followed the rules. Once, though, he was very upset with the officials and he followed them into their dressing room after the game telling them what he thought. Well, of course there is a provision in the league constitution that prohibits a coach from doing this and when the matter was reported to me I knew I had to do something. In Vinnie's case I thought about what he'd done and the degree of its severity and I thought about it for a long time. I finally thought that there is a way of disciplining Vinnie that'd be much more effective than saying: you are fined X number of dollars. So I wrote him a letter and the theme of it was that I was amazed and shocked to learn of his actions after the game. I said I was shocked because they came from a man who is so personally dedicated to authority and respect for order. I told him I felt it was totally out of line with what he stood for. In a subsequent phone conversation I discovered the letter had a tremendous impact on him. He felt very sheepish. The letter had hurt him and it had had its effect. It was far more effective than if I'd fined him $5,000.

MARK DUNCAN: In one game he jumped all over an official. He laced him something terrible on the sideline and on Monday or Tuesday he called me and he said, "Mark, I gotta ask you to do something. I want you to apologize to the official for me." He said, "I won't see him for a while and I jumped all over this man and I found out in the films yesterday that he was absolutely right."

CHUCK JOHNSON: He would terminate a press conference because of what he thought was a stupid question. He'd say, "That's it!"

SAM HUFF: Once he got off the bus after a great post-game tirade and he said, "You know, I'm so damn mean I scare myself!"

GEORGE HALAS: Lombardi didn't surprise or confound you. He just beat you. I remember commenting to a reporter after a loss to Green Bay: "They didn't do anything we didn't expect. But we couldn't stop them from doing it."

¶ He wasn't unbeatable, of course, but you could not start thinking about it on Monday and expect to win over Green Bay the following Sunday. To compete with Lombardi on any Sunday afternoon, you had to work just as hard and intelligently as Lombardi all year long. One thing about playing Lombardi -- you never had to worry about your players being over-confident.

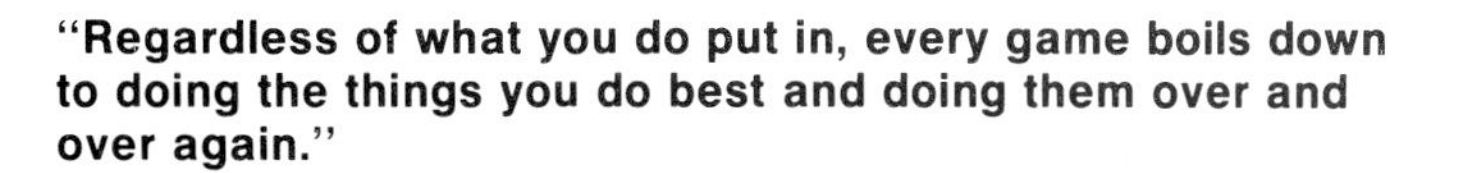

"Regardless of what you do put in, every game boils down to doing the things you do best and doing them over and over again."

Beginnings

"Contrary to the opinion of many people,
leaders are not born.
Leaders are made,
and they are made by effort and hard work."

Vince Lombardi, 1935

"Mental toughness is many things. It is humility, because I think it behooves all of us to remember that simplicity is the sign of all greatness and meekness is the sign of true strength. Mental toughness is Spartanism with those qualities of sacrifice, self-denial, dedication. It is fearlessness and it is love."

Beginnings: the first 45 years

VINCE LOMBARDI, JR: My father really felt uncomfortable about his induction into the Hall of Fame at Fordham. He was one of the first inductees, along with Alex Wojciechowicz, Frankie Frisch and Tom Courtney. He didn't feel as if he belonged to that group because he'd been just an average athlete. He told me, "As far as I'm concerned they're just cheapening this award."

ALEX WOJCIECHOWICZ: He *always* was a winner. He couldn't see us doing anything else *but* winning at Fordham. He never had any doubt we would come out on top – no matter who we were playing.

JIM LAWLOR: Every guy on the first or second team got two tickets. He always gave one to his father and I gave one to my father. So we each always had one left. I was going with a girl on Long Island, where I lived, and also one in the Bronx. They didn't know about each other, of course. I'd always give my other ticket to the girl from Long Island and Vince would give his – which was a seat right next to mine – to Marie. They were going together then. One day Marie couldn't go and without telling me a word he gave his ticket to the girl from the Bronx. So we came out for warmups and we're behind the goal posts throwing blocks at each other and I glanced up in the stands and then I said to him, "You goddamn son of a bitch!," and he took off running down the field laughing as hard as he could laugh. After the game I didn't know what to do. I was the last one out of the shower and when I dressed and came outside there was no one there. I never saw either girl again.

Jim Lawlor   Vince Lombardi   Leo Paquin

CHUCK JOHNSON: He loved to talk about the series Fordham had with Pitt when he was there. In this one game the Fordham quarterback called the same play over and over and over. It was through tackle on Lombardi's side. This Pitt lineman – one of the Matisi brothers – would belt him across the mouth with his forearm on every play. Vince said that finally he staggered back to the huddle with the blood running out of his mouth and he said to the quarterback, "For Christ's sake, can't you call anything else?" He needed a lot of stitches in his mouth after the game.

FATHER KEVIN O'BRIEN: In later years he heartily enjoyed the fact that Andy Palau, the Fordham quarterback, continually called for the play in which Vince had to block on Matisi, the Pittsburgh tackle. And then he would show us the stitch scars on his lower lip – to show that maybe it wasn't quite as enjoyable on that afternoon at the Polo Grounds as he made it out to be.

LEAH LEVITAS: He told us once about this very elaborate plan he made to sneak out of the dorm at Fordham, past the hall monitors. He and his friend succeeded, too, but when they got outside Vince turned to his buddy and said, "Well, here we are with no money and no place to go. What do we do now?" They had to sneak back *into* the dorm.

JIM LAWLOR: They knew about the craps games we'd have in our room and we'd be raided once a month by Father Mulqueen. He would dash in the door, grab every dime on the bed and say, "It's going to missions." The last time we were back at Fordham together, Vince gets an idea and we go to Father Mulqueen and ask him for all our money back he raided from us.

¶ Brother Quinn was in charge of the dining hall. He also was in charge of giving out the jobs there and he turned down Vince and Vince resented it. He told me, "I'm going to get even with that Irish bastard." So just as we were about to leave the dining hall one night, Vince takes a piece of bread and he butters it just as thick as he could get it. Now Brother Quinn was bald and there he was with his big bald head standing outside the dining room. He used to insult the athletes. He'd say, "Here they come! Here come the hogs to the trough!" So Vince had this piece of buttered bread which he had behind his back and got between the five of us – we were all over 6 feet so he couldn't be seen in the middle – and as we passed the dining hall entrance he just stuck his arm out and stuck the buttered bread right on top of Brother Quinn's bald head. The old guy just about died. He never did find out who did it.

¶ He was quite sensitive about being Italian. We went to a sorority dance once and the minute we got in there he could feel the resentment. They had the dance in the main ballroom of this place and you came up the stairs through a foyer into the ballroom. We had gone to the men's room and he was about two steps in front of me and there were five brothers standing by the door and one of them said, "Who's the little Guinea?," and I don't think he even broke stride. He just turned around and let it fly and this guy's teeth disappeared down his throat and the other four brothers jumped in and I jumped in. We had about five minutes of fun and frolic up on the foyer. I told Vince, "We better get out of here." He said, "You're damn right we better," and we grabbed our coats and we were going down the main stairway when two cops were coming up. They said, "Where's the fight, fellows?," and Vince said, "Right up there," and the two of us took off out the door.

¶ On graduation day he was the only one out of a class of 350 who wore white shoes. So I asked him, "Why in hell are you wearing white shoes?," and he said, "Because I *like* white shoes."

¶ You know, his ambitions were to be a businessman and mine were to be a coach.

VINCE LOMBARDI, JR.: He really was a soft touch. When he got out of school, out of Fordham, in the depression days he got a job working for Seaboard Finance or something like that. He'd have to go out to foreclose loans. You can imagine what it must have been like then. He'd go out to see the people about the money they owed and end up giving them cash out of his own pocket.

FATHER TIMOTHY MOORE: Oh, he was tough. Some of the students at St. Cecilia's were a little afraid of him. In fact, sometimes *I* was a little afraid of him.

¶ He was the first football coach in our county and maybe in New Jersey to use the T-formation. While he was at St. Cecilia's, from 1942 to 1946, we played 51 games and we won 39 and tied 5. We had a winning streak of 25 games and an unbeaten streak of 32 games, and 22 of our players were named to all-county and all-state teams. In 1943 his team gave up only 19 points while scoring 267. And then there was basketball, in which he had had little experience. His 1944-45 team won the New Jersey Class A title and during his years in that sport he had nine players on all-county and all-state teams.

¶ Believe this if you like – and it's a gospel fact: when he started here his salary was $1,700 a year; when he left it was $3,500. During the last two summers with us he worked for my oldest brother in road construction. He did a marvelous job as foreman and my brother offered him a job that paid $50,000 a year to stay on with him. He asked me, "What should I do?," and I told him what he *would* do – stay in football.

JOHN DE GASPERIS: During football camp at St. Cecilia's, Coach was out with Father Tim and our trainer Tom Markham. It was late at night and we were supposed to be sleeping. But a few of us got some corn flakes and spread them in their beds. Around midnight, when they went to bed, they discovered the corn flakes. It was hilarious and we heard them laugh but we ended up having a midnight calisthenics drill in our pajamas. It never happened again.

¶ We had a tackle named Norval Dobbs at St. Cecilia's who had eleven boils under his arm. Coach looked at the boils, put some ointment on them and had Norval ready for practice. At one point during a tough block, Norval let out a scream. Coach looked at him and there was a stillness on the field. For the rest of practice Norval didn't make a sound – but believe me, he was in some kind of pain. He didn't miss a practice and he played in the next game.

¶ I played guard and linebacker for him in 1943, when I was a freshman, and after the season I was accidentally shot by a friend of mine with a .22-caliber bullet. I spent 18 days in the hospital and every doctor told me my playing days were over. Father Tim and the coach visited me several times. Coach Lombardi told me the doctors said I wouldn't be playing any more football but that they were wrong. He said I'd be in uniform the next year. The bullet was never removed and I played football not only in high school but also in prep school. In 1951 I captained the University of Delaware team.

FATHER TIMOTHY MOORE: Brooklyn Prep had a line that averaged over 195 – that was big then – and they also had Joe Paterno and his brother in the backfield. A lot of people said that they were the best high high school team in the East. Vince outsmarted them – pure and simple, that's just what he did – and we won 19-7.

JOHN DE GASPERIS: I spoke at an affair given for him

Vince Lombardi, 1947

at the Bergen County Coaches Association a few years ago and before it started Al Quilici, a halfback on our St. Cecilia's team, and myself were in another room talking with Coach Lombardi. Al had said to Coach Lombardi how surprised he was that Coach Lombardi remembered his name after 20 years. And with that, Coach Lombardi told us about the Englewood and Saints game where Al did not down a kickoff by Englewood and an Englewood player downed the ball and went in to score seconds before the game ended to beat us.

FATHER TIMOTHY MOORE: At St. Cecilia's, we shared a two-desk office and he would often say, "Tim, I want to go to confession." He would kneel down beside my desk then and I would hear his confession.

VINCE LOMBARDI, JR.: His concentration was amazing. When he was coaching at St. Cecilia's and driving home there would be times when he'd miss the exit and drive 10 miles before he realized what the hell he'd done. And funniest of all – our area was a lot of tract houses, post-World War II, and they all looked pretty much the same with a small garage in back. There were a lot of times when he'd park the car in a garage two or three doors away and then walk into a strange house.

DICK BOURGUIGNON: The story is told about the time when he had to go somewhere on the train on football business and Marie couldn't take him. This was when he was at West Point. So one of the other assistant coaches at Army took him to the station and when he got out of the car, he kissed the coach goodbye and got on the train. He never knew he did it!

MARIE LOMBARDI: What Vince really wanted out of life was to be head coach at Fordham. He wanted to rebuild Fordham's football back to what it was in the days when he had been there.

ED BRESLIN: He had two great ambitions in life. He wanted to be head coach at Fordham and he wanted to be head coach of the Giants.

MURRAY WARMATH: We started at West Point together in 1949 and I was there for three years and he was there for five. We shared an office together and because we both were civilians we were together quite a bit. You know I honestly don't remember that we ever talked about anything besides football. We must have, I guess, but I don't remember it.

EARL BLAIK: Vinnie brought a lot of things to Army – it was obvious right away that he was a diamond

Vince Lombardi Earl Blaik Murray Warmath

in the rough – but he took some things away, too. Our playbook – the Army method – was a simple one, with a lot of power sweeps. I always believed that the playbooks with 300 plays or variations of plays were basically a lot of baloney. Vinnie carried that same theory to the pros and he used it well through all the days at Green Bay.

¶ Another West Point theory that served him well was that of attacking an opponent's strength. The Michigan team of '49 had won 22 or 23 games in a row and they were coming off a great performance in the Rose Bowl. The game was in Yost Stadium and we had no chance. We went after their tackle, Wistert, a big hulking guy, smashing him low on every play. In the end he could hardly walk and we had won by 21-7. Vinnie always said that that one game proved to him that nothing is impossible.

MURRAY WARMATH: He felt prejudice, I'm sure of that. He felt that because he was Italian and Catholic that he was not going to be hired by a southern school and a few others, too. And like me, there was nothing else on his mind except being a head coach somewhere.

RAY BILOTTI: He used to love to tell this story about when he was running the offense at West Point. There was this guy whose name I forget and apparently the other guards on the team and the people who followed football didn't feel that this fellow was qualified to learn offense. But Lombardi started him anyway. Of course everybody was saying that the only reason Lombardi started this fellow was because he was Italian. And Lombardi said – and he would roar when he told this story – "I didn't start the S.O.B. because *he's* an Italian. I started him because *I'm* an Italian!"

EARL BLAIK: The cribbing scandal in 1951 hit us all hard but it really tore at Vince. Our football team was virtually wiped out and we had to scramble like hell to field any kind of team at all. One of our opponents was Northwestern and we had no business being on the same field with them. Well, we led them by 14-13 when they scored a touchdown on a long pass in the final minute and beat us 20-14. It was a great game, an impossible effort, and we'd come so damn close. Vince sat in that locker room when it was over and he cried like a baby.

¶ When the Giants fired Steve Owen after the 1953 season they had to placate the press so they came to me. It was a fantastic offer, I must admit, but I felt I had to turn it down. So I told Well Mara, "Why don't you talk to my man Vince?" Mara knew all about Vinnie – they were classmates at Fordham – and my encouragement was all he needed. He offered Vince over $5,000 a year more to go to the Giants as an assistant. Vince was reluctant to accept it. What he wanted then was to be a head coach in college.

WELLINGTON MARA: We had just hired Jim Lee Howell as coach in '54 and we were thinking about adding Vinnie to the staff. We sent him to Jim Lee's ranch in Arkansas so the two of them could talk. Jim Lee raised cattle and steers and his first conversation with Vince there was in a pen, with animals moving all around them. Vinnie had never been anywhere in his life, really, except New York and New Jersey. He said later, "It takes a lot to scare me but one thing that'll do it every time is anything that walks on four legs and is bigger than me!"

JIM LEE HOWELL: He was very quiet, very inward, when he came down to my place in Lonoke. I remember what opened him up, though. A friend of mine had shot some wild ducks and he brought them over and my mother-in-law cooked up a meal of wild duck, wild rice and a lot of things like that. He just couldn't believe it and he kept saying over and over, "You can't *buy* anything like this anywhere."

WELLINGTON MARA: His first day in camp with us, in 1954, I walked around the back of the room while he ran down the cadences. Even the guys in the back row were listening. The rafters shook, I'll tell you.

TOM LANDRY: He came out of college as a good football coach. He was competent but he wasn't sure. It took him a year or so. It took him one year to establish himself in pro football and understand what was going on.

JIM LEE HOWELL: Our coaching staff then was a democracy, in the truest sense of the word. I encouraged an outpouring of feelings and theories. Some rivalries developed as a result of this but I guess it was only natural that two strong men like Vince Lombardi and Tom Landry would be at odds. Vinnie ran the offense and Tom ran the defense and that meant they went head-on in practice. One day one of them would come in and tell me he hadn't been given enough time and the next day the other would. One would say his unit wasn't being worked hard enough; the other would say just the opposite. They were fussing all the time.

FRANK GIFFORD: When he came to us from West Point he had a lot to learn. He knew the running game, sure, but the pro passing game was different. He'd come to our room – Charlie Conerly and I were roomies – and we'd talk football for hours, drinking beer and trading theories. Vince was just one of the guys. It was funny, I remember that there were a lot of things that Vince said that first year that we never really took seriously. He put in some razzle-dazzle option that Charlie never called and there were some plays he had from the Army days. He also had a belly series that was just too complex. The pros played it a little more direct then.

¶ We were a tough team and I think a lot of that rubbed off on him. Like Conerly. Once he broke his nose during a game and it was a real mess. Charlie called consecutive timeouts – you could do that then – and they pushed the nose around and he stayed in the game. Vinnie loved it when a man'd show courage like that. With the Packers, though, it wasn't a matter of choice. He demanded that courage.

WELLINGTON MARA: He was very restless. He wore his heart on his sleeve. After the '54 season with us he came and told my brother Jack and I that he was going back to Army. We talked him out of doing that but there were continuous lures after that. From the start of the '57 season – and maybe a little bit before that – he became a desirable commodity to other clubs.

JIM LEE HOWELL: The oldest of the Mara brothers, Jack, was a fan of horse racing. When we were leaving one time to go down to Philadelphia for the draft, Vinnie leaned into Jack's office and said, "We're going down to Philadelphia to get the horses." And Jack said, "There are a lot of good horses around but a good horse isn't worth a damn with a poor jockey."

FRANK GIFFORD: We used to kid the hell out of him, you know, never letting him forget about St. Cecilia's and West Point and Fordham. Once somebody dug up a picture of the Seven Blocks of Granite in those funny stances of theirs and it broke us up. There was a game we played called Sports Quiz and the idea was that someone would do a famous athlete and the rest of the guys would try to guess who it was. So once our entire offensive line would get down in that funny old-fashioned stance and yell, "Sports Quiz! Sports Quiz!"

EMLEN TUNNELL: Me and Rosey Brown were roomies and one year when we were training in Salem, Oregon, we went into Portland. Well, we couldn't get back. Just couldn't get a ride. So I said, "Roomie, we might as well stay out all night because there's no way else." When we finally did get back there it was 5 o'clock in the morning and the sun's not even coming up yet. And there's Vinnie sitting on the steps. He'd been waiting there all night for Rosey to come back. He didn't care about me. I was a defensive player.

ROSEY BROWN: He was sitting on the steps there and he said, "You okay?," and I said, "Fine," and he said, "What happened?" Emlen said, "We couldn't get a taxi." Which was the gospel truth. So we went up to bed. We never got fined. He could have reported us. It could have cost us $250 or something like that.

VINCE LOMBARDI, JR.: Jim Lee threw me off the field one time. I was bringing out water or balls or something and I was late. A couple of other guys were late for practice and they came out at the same time. Jim Lee asked me who the late players were and I wouldn't tell him and he said, "Get off the field until you remember." I left but I was worried about what my father's reaction would be. I avoided him for days after that. But when I finally ran into him he said, "I would have killed you if you had told on those guys."

SAM HUFF: We were up in training camp in Burlington, Vermont, our first year and Don Chandler and I, we were just country boys who were homesick. One day Chandler says to me, "Let's get the hell out of this place," and I said, "Yeah, let's go." I'd hurt my knee anyway, chasing Buddy Young in practice. And so we went to turn in our playbooks and take off. We looked for Jim Lee Howell but we couldn't find him so we went to Lombardi's room. He was asleep on the couch when we walked in so I said, "Coach," kinda loud, and he jumped up and said, "What the hell do *you* want?" And I said, "We're quitting," and he flew into a rage. Well, Chandler got out of there – me, I had my bad knee so I couldn't run – and Coach screamed and yelled at me – backed me against the wall – and called me every name in the book. He said, "You're not going to quit on me!" So I stayed and they got Chandler at the airport. He lasted 13 years in the pros and I went 14.

FRANK GIFFORD: Things would get to be a drag in workouts and we'd cut the distance between units by crowding the workout area. One unit would be right on the tail of the other and it would cut down the room you'd have to run to get up to the line of scrimmage. Vinnie would get mad and he'd put down an orange peel and he'd announce that he wanted each unit to stay behind the peel until their turn. So we'd push the orange peel forward a little bit when he wasn't looking. Then a little more. Then a little more. After a few plays we'd be right back where we were before. Oh, he'd get furious. But then he'd laugh right along with the rest of us.

JIM LEE HOWELL: He was very patient. He would go to great lengths to teach, especially any individual who had promise. The thing that he would not tolerate, that would really upset him, was when a player who had promise let him down – if they failed to do what they were taught. One time when a player he liked and respected had this new play down pat and in practice all week he ran it perfectly. Vince was delighted. Then, on Saturday, in our last dress rehearsal, we ran the play over and the player botched it up totally. Vince said, very loudly, "You sure messed that up, mister," and the two of them shouted back and forth until finally the player said, "I think the heat's got you." Well, you can imagine! He ended up by chasing the player down the field. Lucky for the player he was faster.

¶ One night before a preseason game in Oregon, I looked out the window of the hotel where we were staying and there was Vince pacing back and forth on the second-floor roof that was outside our rooms. He was so intense. We always kidded him after that. When he'd get excited we'd say, "Someone go find a roof for Vinnie."

¶ When the other coaches – the rest of us – would leave the Giant offices, there always was one light still burning, the one in Vince Lombardi's office.

CHUCK BEDNARIK: I knew Vince from a couple of Pro Bowls when Jim Lee Howell was the head coach. I really liked him. In fact I heard once, in '58 I think it was, that he was the No. 1 candidate to coach us in Philly. I really hoped he'd get the job.

PAT SUMMERALL: We were training out in Salem, Oregon, that year, in 1958, and I went to the first offensive meeting and I can remember asking whoever was sitting

Jim Lee Howell

next to me — I think it was Don Heinrich —
"Who the hell is that guy?" because the guy had such
an obvious complete command of what he was saying and
he had everything down to how long the first
step ought to be, how deep the guards ought to pull
and, you know, everything like that. It was Lombardi and
I'll tell you: He wasn't a backfield coach; he wasn't
a line coach, and he wasn't a receiver coach.
He was the coach of the offense and he knew every part
of the machine — what the ends were supposed
to do, what blocks the tackles and guards ought to call.
Just a complete command of what he was teaching.
What a great teacher he was! I'm sure that in
school or wherever you go nine people could say
the same thing but the way that one of them
says it makes it stick in your mind far better.

WELLINGTON MARA: We had a veteran team in '58 and
it had a lousy preseason. The players were overtired and
I heard reports that they thought they'd been
driven too hard. We were scheduled to open the season
in Buffalo against the Cardinals and things went
from bad to worse. Half the team was hurt — a lot of
linemen were out — and it looked like the end
of the world. On the Tuesday before the game we had
dinner with Vince and Marie. He left early to
go to a team meeting and after he'd gone Marie said,
"You ever see a sick cat get well?," and I said,
"Not one this sick."

¶ John Martin was the host there at Bear Mountain
and he was a good friend of Vince's. They got together
and agreed that what the guys needed was a good
time. So they got Jim Lee Howell and I out of
camp and brought in an orchestra and some kegs of beer.
You would think that something like that would
tire a guy out even more but it actually had an
opposite effect. We flew to Buffalo on Saturday morning
and everybody ran so fast — literally flew —
in the workouts that practice was cut off after 20
minutes. I remember going back to the Statler to watch
a college game on TV and thinking there's no
way we could lose. And then I looked over and I knew
for sure. There was Vinnie, shoes off, feet up,
fast asleep. We beat the hell out of the Cardinals.

KYLE ROTE: He threw a beer party for us one year at
Bear Mountain when Jim Lee was away. The
idea was to loosen us up. The next day one of our
halfbacks was trying to field a punt but his bloodshot
eyes couldn't quite focus on the ball and it hit
him right on the top of the head. We wondered

about the effects of the beer party then but we found out about its effects later. We had a winning season.

ROSEY BROWN: I had a depressed fracture of the cheekbone in '58. We'd tried out a lot of helmets to see if they'd fit properly over the cheekbone but none of them worked. So Vinnie went home and got one of those old helmets, the leather kind that he used to wear at Fordham. He brought it to the stadium and he said, "Maybe you could use this." It fit but I wouldn't have dared played in that thing. The point is, though, that the guy was always thinking.

PAT SUMMERALL: I remember a game against the Browns that we won when I kicked a long field goal right at the end, in the snow. When Jim Lee Howell called for me and the field goal unit Lombardi was shaking his head. He didn't want to try it but it was damn near the only move we had. There were less than two minutes left and we weren't moving the ball. Anyway, we made it. I was walking back off the field and one of the people I encountered on the sidelines was Lombardi. He just looked at me with that big alligator grin of his and said, "You know, don't you, that you can't really kick it that far?!"

ED BRESLIN: After the '58 season he told me he'd like to work for us, for Federation Bank and Trust, so we set a sales deal up where he got $175 a week. He was really pleased with that. And he did well, too. He could sell. Mostly, he wasn't afraid to work. He started on a Monday and on the first Thursday I noticed him in a teller's cage and I went over and I said, "What the hell you doing in here?," and he said, "I finished my calls. I wanted to see how this works."

¶ A lot of things were going on then. The West Point job opened up when Col. Blaik resigned and he wanted that. But he told me "I don't think I can get it. My name ends in a vowel." And then two weeks after he started with the bank Marie called me on Sunday and said, "I'm sworn to secrecy but can you cover for Vince tomorrow?" I wanted to know what was going on. It wasn't until Tuesday when I found out. Vince called me in the afternoon and said he'd just got back into town from Green Bay and he wanted to talk with me. He had tears in his eyes when he told me he'd taken the job. Then we went out and walked around New York. I said, "It's what you've always wanted," and he said, "Yeah, and the first thing I'm gonna do out there is build a defense."

Winning

"The will to excel and the will to win, they endure.
They are more important than any events that occasion them."

68
44

"It is becoming increasingly difficult to be tolerant of a society that has sympathy only for misfits, only for the maladjusted, only for the criminal, only for the loser. Have sympathy for them. Help them. But I think it's also time for all of us to stand up and cheer for the doer, the achiever, the one who recognizes a problem and does something about it, one who looks for something extra to do for his country —the winner, the leader."

Winning: the last 12 years

DOMENIC OLEJNICZAK: When I asked George Halas about him he said, "I shouldn't tell you this, Ole, but he'll be a good one. I shouldn't tell you because you're liable to kick the crap out of us!"

DICK BOURGUIGNON: We must have called the Maras, I don't know how many times, for permission to talk to Lombardi. In the meantime, he had expressed his desire to talk to us. But every time we talked to the Maras they said, "How about Tom Landry?" They kept pushing Tom over Vince all the time. We called Paul Brown and he said, "As far as I'm concerned Lombardi is the top coach in football today. He is the guts and brains of the Giants club."

JERRY ATKINSON: I got ahold of Paul Brown and he said, "Lombardi is a great football tactician and he also is a scrapper. He'll get the most out of his men. He won't let anybody dog him." And then he said, "But you'll never get him," and I said, "Why?," and Brown said, "Well, because he's married to the Maras. They have a $100,000 life insurance policy on him and he has virtually a lifetime contract. Also he's connected with some bank there and, mostly, he's a New Yorker and you just don't take New Yorkers out of New York. I know I rarely even hire one for our business here because they just have a heckuva time adjusting." So I said, "But if we could get him, Paul, would he be the right man?," and Brown said, "He certainly would be." I said, "We want a Paul Brown of Green Bay. Would you be willing to work closely with him and assist us in setting it up?" Brown said he would. In that first year, we got Henry Jordan,

Willie Davis, Bill Quinlan and Lew Carpenter from Cleveland. I'll never forget Paul Brown for what he did for us, for Green Bay.

DICK BOURGUIGNON: So we met him, Tony Canadeo and I, for the first time, just after he got off the plane, and we asked him how free he was. And he said, "Before I left, Jack Mara told me, 'Let your good judgment and training be your guide.' " He told us he'd graduated from Fordham. So I said to him, "I graduated from Marquette and I've got that good judgment and training." And Canadeo, who happened to be sitting on the other side of Lombardi, said, "I graduated from Gonzaga and I've got that good judgment and training, too." And Lombardi said, "Between the three of us Jesuits here, we could kick the shit out of these non-Catholics!" He said, "We are going to get along." It was as if we had been friends for a long time.

¶ The timing was perfect. It was being in the right place at the right time. Green Bay had gone through such trials and tribulations and bad years that it was really ripe for someone to come in. But fate also gave us the man who was just right for that situation.

JERRY ATKINSON: Lombardi came out here the day before Christmas and we sat down to talk. I turned over a place mat and I said, "Let's write 'em down"—the positives for his coming to Green Bay. "No. 1, money. It doesn't compare. You'd do better in Green Bay. No. 2, autonomy. It doesn't compare, of course. No. 3, talent. It doesn't compare. You've got a young club here. No. 4, national acclaim. The Giants have no place to go but to stay up or go down and the Packers can go up. Also it would be like working with David against all the Goliaths here. And No. 5, home, living conditions. We can match anybody in those."

WELLINGTON MARA: I gave the Packer people permission to talk to him and he went out there. He really was gung-ho when he came back and he told me that not only had he taken the job but that he'd already leased a house. He told me he'd spent the whole morning at mass that day meditating. I was the only person who knew he'd taken the job — not even Marie knew — and that night there was a Fordham alumni banquet. Marie was there and she pleaded with me not to let him go. He still had one more year to go on his assistant's contract and legally I could have kept him. I told her that morally I felt I had to let Vinnie do what he wanted. I knew what that was.

¶ The way we figured it, Jim Lee Howell was going to go on coaching the Giants for a long time. That's really why we agreed to let Vinnie go to Green Bay — and why a five-year contract for him didn't seem constricting. Late in 1959, Vinnie's first year away from us, I could see that the bloom was gone from Jim Lee and I asked him. He said he was tired of coaching. So I called Vinnie and told him the Giants' job was his. He said he would feel guilty leaving Green Bay after one year, to wait another and then the time would be right. So Jim Lee stayed on through 1960 but then Vinnie won the Western title that season and there was just no way he could have come East.

VINCE LOMBARDI, JR.: I never will forget that ride out from New York, the four of us in the car. My mother was crying and so was I and my sister. He tried to make things happy. He tried to make us laugh. "It's cold," he said, "but it's a dry cold." Already he sounded like a Chamber of Commerce.

CHUCK JOHNSON: He was beautiful with the press that year. I'll never forget my first meeting. He was in Green Bay for a morning press conference and I drove up there from Milwaukee, through a terrible snow and ice storm. It was slow driving and I got there late. Lombardi was doing television interviews when I arrived so I told Tom Miller, the P-R man then, that I'd be in the restaurant eating lunch, that he should bring the coach in when he was through on television. A few minutes later he came in and we shook hands for the first time. I asked a lot of questions and since I was still eating I didn't take any notes. Then I drove back to Milwaukee and wrote my story. Well, a week later he came to Milwaukee for the first time and when I encountered him he was with Miller again and Tom said, "You remember Chuck Johnson, don't you?" And he said, "Do I remember Chuck Johnson?! He wrote that nice story last week and he didn't take a note." He said it so loud everyone in the room heard it. And you know that's the last time he ever said a nice thing about anything I wrote about him or his team until 1968, when he was general manager.

TOM FEARS: When I first went up there I took my oldest son, Pat. I thought he'd stay with me in my hotel or whatever. But Vince and Marie took him in and kept him about four months, until my whole family moved up. He lived there and Marie used to take him to school. But after he got you situated, he created a gap between you and him. It was strictly business after that.

"You will be proud of the team because I will be proud of the team."

RED COCHRAN: When I moved my family to Green Bay from Detroit I had a 22-month and a 2-month pair of baby girls. The house we bought included a stove, refrigerator, studio couch, regular couch, kitchen table and chairs. Thus it was livable and more convenient with the babies than a motel while we waited for our furniture to arrive. The wait stretched on, too, because of a severe snowstorm. Vince and Marie came by on a Sunday afternoon, expecting to see us all moved in because he knew our moving schedule. When they walked into that bare house and he saw Pat and me and those two babies his first words were, "Come on, you are coming home with us." So off they took us. We stayed with them a week.

BOYD DOWLER: I always thought of him only as the head coach in Green Bay. I know that sounds funny but it just seemed like all of a sudden he appeared from nowhere in Green Bay. It was like that was what he always was and there weren't any other earlier years in his life. The minute I saw him in 1959 I knew who he was. It really was strange. He was an overwhelming inspiration from the beginning.

BOB SKORONSKI: I remember very well our first meeting at St. Norbert College. Everyone was apprehensive because we had heard a lot of things and we knew that he had not been a head coach. We were wondering if this was really the guy who was going to save the Packers. So he got up and said, "You may not be a football player. You may not be a tackle. You may not be a guard. You may not be a back. But you *will* be a professional." I believe very sincerely that that statement had more to do with making champions of us than anything he did as Packer coach.

BILL FORESTER: His first talk to the squad at the start of training camp, before he was through chills were running up and down your spine, your hands were sweaty and you were ready to go outside and scrimmage without pads. He got me so keyed up I could hardly sleep that night.

MAX MC GEE: His first speech to the whole squad is famous now, where he told everybody that we had two options: We could stay there and pay the price for winning or else we could get the hell out. The next day he came over to me and he looked relieved. He said that he'd been nervous as hell about giving that speech. He said he didn't know if he'd have two people left the next day. He was afraid the whole squad might leave him. But no one did.

EMLEN TUNNELL: On the first day of practice he told

Dave Hanner and Tom Bettis and Jerry Helluin to lose 20 pounds in two weeks or get the hell out of camp. Helluin was the only one who didn't do it and he got cut. Hanner was fat and it damn near killed him to lose that weight. But it probably added those last six years to his career.

HENRY JORDAN: When he came here we were losers. We were out-of-shape losers. He got us into superb condition. We couldn't believe how hard he was working us. But he was right. If you're in shape physically you can be mentally tough also.

TOM BETTIS: The first week of training camp, the trainer's room was filled with players getting treatment for minor injuries. He cleared the room one day and from that day on there was a different mood on the team, a Spartan mood.

EMLEN TUNNELL: He just took charge of everything right away. This team had been down in the dumps. They didn't travel first class. They stayed in lousy hotels and they even had box lunches. He changed all that. He made those guys feel like pros. The guys who'd been around there before he came, they didn't know what that was like.

¶ It was bad for blacks, too. Real bad. Nate Borden was the only black player on the team when he came and Nate was staying in a place where I wouldn't have kept my dog. Vinnie changed all that. He gave the people who were renting the room to Nate hell and then he moved him into a decent place. There were never any second-class citizens on the Packers, black or white.

¶ In the first meeting we had on the field, he called us all together – about 60 guys – and he said, "If I ever hear nigger or dago or kike or anything like that around here, regardless of who you are, you're through with me. You can't play for me if you have any kind of prejudice." I think deep down there is always going to be some prejudice but as long as you don't feel it as a group you are going to do all right.

JIMMY CANNON: His dignity and grace in racial matters was almost totally neglected. It was so sincere, so natural, that it passed unnoticed. In his own way, he was a great social scientist. He made black and white people some neutral color.

MAX MC GEE: The year before he got there everybody was out playing for his own contract and doing what would individually satisfy himself. But after Lombardi came everybody on the squad worked

for the team, I'm convinced of it. I played many games where they didn't throw me the ball but maybe once I threw a little block for Taylor and we won the game so I was happy.

JIM RINGO: One of his first speeches was, "We are going to run. We are going to block. We are going to tackle. We are going to play football."

BOB SKORONSKI: I remember the first year that he said, "Fatigue makes cowards of us all." There were a lot of guys around that day and some of them laughed and giggled. But you know, four or five years later those same guys who giggled, I heard them say to some young players, bonus babies: "Hey, you had better get moving or fatigue will make cowards of you."

LOU SPADIA: I'd always taken a great interest in game programs and I guess I got to be known as the ranking expert on them around the league. When Vince went to Green Bay in '59, he really picked my brains about game programs. He wanted to know all about game programs. He wanted to know all about them – about rates, about everything. Then we found out that the Packers had been charging advertisers $250 a page when it cost the club $600. He changed that.

¶ He was never too proud to ask a question. He'd say, "I don't understand it. Explain it to me."

SAM HUFF: We played the Packers in a preseason game in Bangor, Maine, in 1959 and Vince came around to our hotel to say hello. He ran into a bunch of us – Gifford and Conerly and Webster and I – in the lobby and he got so choked up he could hardly talk.

DAD BRAISHER: The first year we made a trip by train. We had lost a couple games, a couple preseason games. I was out in the vestibule of the coach smoking a cigarette and he came out there and he was upset – not over the fact that we had lost so much as he knew we had a losing complex and he was worried we wouldn't get over it.

EMLEN TUNNELL: I'd kid him about his monogrammed shirts. I'd say, "I remember when you were an assistant coach with the Giants. You only had a couple shirts then."

DUDS BILOTTI: The first time we met he walked in with his knickers and green jacket. Walked right in the place off the practice field. We were unpacking boxes – we hadn't opened yet – and my cousin Danny was behind the bar getting the bar set up. And Vince walked in with his cap on and I don't know what he said but my cousin Danny, who didn't know anything about

football or baseball, yelled, "We're not open yet." And then Danny yelled to us – my brother and me – "Who the hell is this guy with the knickers?" Now Vince was starting to steam up and he yelled, "Any Bilottis around?" So we came out, real quick like, gave him a little tour and made coffee for him. Then he ran back to the field.

DOMENIC OLEJNICZAK: We gave him a five-year contract at $36,000 a year – which was just what he wanted. We ended up ripping that up and writing it over three times before he left. There were bonuses, too, and when we talked to him about them originally we told him there'd be so much for first place, so much for second, so much for third. He asked if we couldn't include the third-place money, which was $5,000, in the first-place figure and we agreed to that. He finished tied for third that first year but we won seven games and he'd done a lot for us. So we gave him a bonus of $10,000. He was so delighted he rushed right out and bought Marie a mink coat.

¶ Wellington Mara had asked for permission to talk to him after the season and we granted it. But I told him, "Just because we're letting you talk to him doesn't mean we'll let you go. I doubt like hell we will." If we'd given our blessing, he'd have gone to New York. I'm sure of it.

FRANK GIFFORD: When I talked with guys from the Packers – like Hornung – I couldn't believe we were talking about the same person. I couldn't believe the fear he instilled in the Packers. He never intimidated the Giants like that. Not once.

FATHER DAVID RONDOU: Every day he would come to 8 o'clock mass but in all the years I knew him, all the years he came here, I never talked football with him once. So many priests, they think because they watch a game they'd say, "Why don't you put in McGee?," or "Is so-and-so hurt?" I figured when he came here he wanted to forget football. So I would talk about my operations – like an old lady I like to talk about operations – and I would ask him to pray for me. We talked about our grade school. It was going downhill then. He even went over there and talked to the students. The sisters were just in love with the guy. They would run up to him – "Mr. Lombardi! Mr. Lombardi!" And they'd ask him questions.

WELLINGTON MARA: When we picked the new commissioner in Miami in 1960 most of us wanted Marshall Leahy for the job. When he wouldn't move east from

San Francisco we looked for a compromise candidate. There were two men mentioned at that point. One of them was Paul Brown. The other was Vince Lombardi. After just two years as a head coach, he already was held in the highest regard.

JIM KENSIL: He really was the first coach to be exposed to a lot of things that hadn't been done before. Like big press conferences and television interviews and tape recorders. He didn't like any of it. But he did it all.

DR. ANTHONY PISONE: Once he held up someone's chest X-ray to look at it and I had to chuckle. I told him, "Every Sunday afternoon your X-rays are seen by millions of people."

CHUCK LANE: The minute the other team made a mistake – as one of the writers said – it was like bleeding in front of a shark. Tex Maule said that a team is a reflection of its head coach. I think the Packers were just that. They were very efficient, just like him.

PAUL HORNUNG: It sounds ludicrous, I know, for me to talk about point spreads but I firmly believe that Lombardi was worth an average of seven points in every game he ever coached.

PAT PEPPLER: His sweep, which is not that great a football play in many ways, put a lot of pressure on the defenses in the early days. It was well designed but that play became good because of Hornung, because he was a great blocker, because he ran where there was daylight, because he could throw the option pass off the sweep.

PAUL HORNUNG: Vince really liked my mother. I don't think she ever saw us lose a game and this didn't pass him unnoticed. Like most people in sports, he was incredibly superstitious. It was because of her that I was invited to the Sunday night cocktail sessions at the Lombardis. I seldom went. I didn't want to isolate myself from the other players. One of the few times I did, though, Lombardi was behind the bar. I rushed over and said, "Just one time, mix me something so I can tell everyone that Coach Lombardi made me a drink." And he said through his teeth to me – he was smiling – "I'll be goddamned if I'll make you a drink," and then he hurried over to my mother.

DICK BOURGUIGNON: He really was superstitious. My wife would have a cocktail party every Friday before a game and there would be just a small group there. He could relax in a small group and he liked that Friday routine. One week Tony Canadeo's wife decided it was her turn to entertain Friday and so she had a nice cocktail party and dinner. We lost the game that Sunday. So when we got to his house on Sunday night, the first thing he says to Canadeo is, "I've got news for you Canadeo. We're not going over to your house before any damn ball games. From now on we're going back to the Bourguignons on Friday." And the next Friday we were back at our place and darned if we didn't beat someone that Sunday. So Vince said,"We can't break the streak." We hosted the Friday cocktail party for the next seven years. He wouldn't let it change.

VINCE LOMBARDI, JR.: His circle of friends in Green Bay were the kissingest bunch. They were always kissing somebody. If they saw somebody in the afternoon, they would kiss them. When he got to know people, well, he was quite a back slapper.

OCKIE KRUEGER: When the Packers split their league schedule with half the games in Milwaukee and half in Green Bay, he gave me complete charge of the Milwaukee part of it. I was not new to sports, of course, but I was new to the NFL and going into a new job certain things frighten you. So I called him in Green Bay and asked him a question about something. I must have called him at the wrong time because he said, "I thought you were gonna run things for me down there in Milwaukee." I said, "Thank you very much." That was the last question I ever asked him in the 11 years I was associated with him.

PAUL MAZZOLENI: I once asked him a question on a minor item. He didn't reply for a moment but then he shot right back and said, "Don't ask any question you can answer yourself"— meaning "think".

MARK DUNCAN: In one game, when I was still coaching in San Francisco, we played the Packers in Milwaukee and we had the ball 33 times in the first half and Green Bay had it 13 times. You know what the score was? 13-7 for the Packers! I swear, they just never made mistakes! They just waited for you to make one and then they'd jump on it.

¶ He just hated his teams to be penalized. I was told that he would fine a player over a penalty — a stupid penalty. He didn't want mistakes of that nature ever. A lot of coaches *say* they don't want them but they still have them anyway. Lombardi worked at preventing them.

EMLEN TUNNELL: I was 38 years old when I left Green Bay in '61 but he asked me if I wanted to stay there. He was always saying he was going to build a dynasty there.

CHUCK BEDNARIK: In '62 I know when they played us that he built up the '60 game to them and made this one kind of a revenge thing. The Packers had just about the same team that year as they did in '60. We had 15, 20 different guys. We weren't the same team by a long shot. Hell, I was 37 and I was set to retire. Well, they beat us that day 49-0. It was the worst physical beating I ever had in the pros.

JIM RINGO: He wouldn't let you make critical errors. If you did, you wouldn't be with him any longer. He couldn't tolerate them. So we felt we would never defeat ourselves. We saw many other teams get in crucial situations, pressure situations, where they would be defeated. Take for instance in 1962, when we came out against the Lions trailing 7-6 with less than a minute to play. Milt Plum made a mistake and threw a turnout to Studstill and Adderley picked it off and we went and got a field goal and won 9-7.

¶ We had quite an offensive team in 1962 and it was supplemented by a great defensive team. We felt we could throw the ball any time we wanted to against any defensive alignment. This was all done through the intelligence and perseverance of Vince. He made us believers.

BOB SKORONSKI: We had the division all wrapped up. We were in San Francisco in '62 and he was so elated with what had happened that year. He wanted to tell us how proud he was that we won and that we had won so early and he really didn't know what to say except how proud he was of us.

JACK TEELE: I never appreciated anything more in my life than when he came out here in 1962 with his ball club and they had clinched the championship. We had sold 60,000 tickets so we weren't worried about that but we were concerned that he would go with a second-string quarterback and other second-line players and that there would be a lot of public criticism. We couldn't afford to offend the L.A. pro football fan. Well, he took his team up to Santa Barbara and he worked the tail off them all week long and he stressed one point: We are the Packers and we are a proud team. The Packer players said they never worked harder.

EDWARD BENNETT WILLIAMS: He and I were down in Miami and we were sitting talking very late one night about the pressures, the terrible pressures of staying

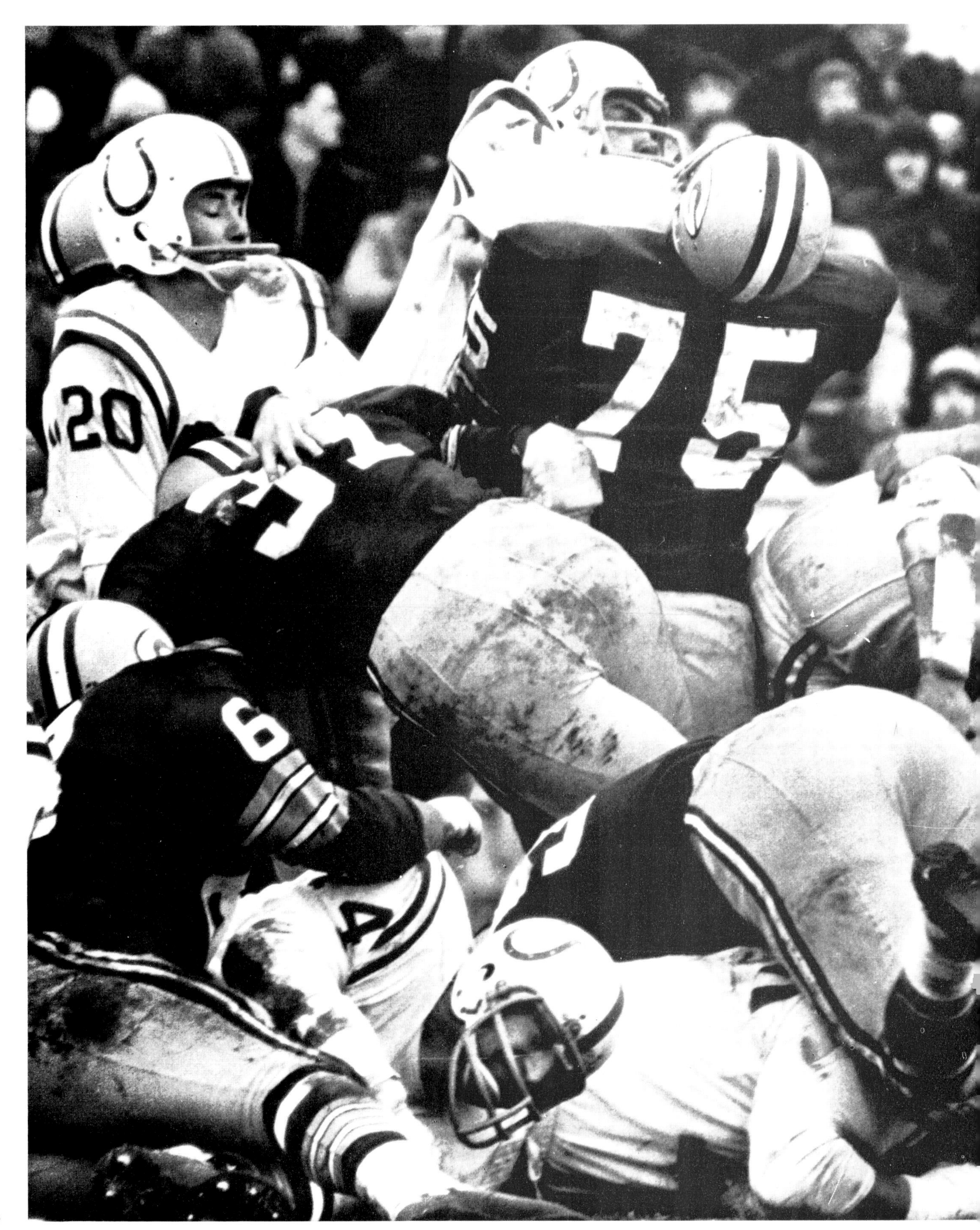
20
75

on top. He had just won his second title, over the Giants. And he was saying how much harder it is to stay there than it is to get there and he said something I've never forgotten: "Success is like a narcotic. One becomes addicted to it but it has a terrible side to it because it saps the elation of victory and deepens the despair of defeat."

PAT SUMMERALL: Before the 1963 season we were sitting around and Harland Svare was quizzing him about what philosophy he should adopt in coaching the Rams, a team that had been down for a long time, a team that had some talent but had never been able to put it together. And he asked Lombardi if he should let them coast a little bit through training camp, let them play themselves into shape, have them at what peak he could get them to when the regular season started or whether he should have them bear down in the preseason games. And Lombardi said, "There's no question in my mind how you have to approach it. You've got to win every game. Just like we did at Green Bay. Because the guys aren't used to winning. They've never tasted it. They don't know what it's like. You've got to try your damnedest to win every game no matter what the importance is because you've got to teach them the winning habit."

ART DALEY: In 1963 Bart Starr broke his hand in St. Louis and Lombardi was particularly vicious with the press. He didn't want to say it was broken. He just wouldn't talk and in the week after he even kicked a photographer off the practice field, fearing he would take a picture of Bart. After the season Vince explained that the reason he acted like that was because "as soon as you make a big thing out of a star player being hurt the entire team can start to feel sorry for itself." Vince would never have let that happen but he was afraid it could.

WILLIE WOOD: We didn't concern ourselves as to what the elements were, the weather conditions. The point is, you've got to play and that's a fact of life. That's what you're here for. And the team that can function best under any conditions comes out victorious.
I remember one year we were going to play the Cleveland Browns down in Miami in the Runnerup Bowl — after the '63 season I think. And we had one of the worst snows up here ever. But instead of going down to Miami we stayed up here and practiced. What difference does it make? It's your job and you gotta do it, no matter where. That was Vince's philosophy: You are being paid by the Green Bay Packers to

play football no matter what conditions are.

PAUL HORNUNG: I think it was in 1964. We were getting ready to go to Minnesota to play the Vikings and the odds favored the Vikings by like 6 or 6½ points. Lombardi had a big grin on his face on the day the odds were announced and he said to us, "I can't remember the last time we were underdogs. Boy, I don't know about you guys but that fires me up." And you know me – I'd just come back from the suspension – and I said, "Yeah, coach. Why don't we get some money together and bet the line?"

HERB ADDERLEY: That runnerup game in 1964, that really galled him. He told us at the beginning of the '65 season that if we didn't win the championship – if we finished second again – that he wasn't going to Miami with us. I don't believe he would have, either.

WILLIE DAVIS: He was so upset with that game that he took an ad out in the Wall Street Journal – paid for it himself, as far as I know. It said: "There is a second-place bowl game but it is a game for losers played by losers."

TEX MAULE: He had this quarterback from Nebraska named Dennis Claridge in '64 and '65 and he tells me that this kid is going to be the greatest thing in the National Football League, that he could play him anywhere – defensive backfield, offensive backfield, even linebacker – and have a genuine star. I didn't agree and I told Vinnie so. He said, "You just watch." After the season Claridge went to Atlanta in the expansion draft and the next time I saw Vinnie I reminded him of it. "Well," he said, "that's one time you were right."

KEN IMAN: When I was traded to the Rams, Lombardi called me personally. His words were, "Hello, Ken. This is Lombardi." There was a moment of silence. "I think you know why I'm calling." I said I did. He sounded very remorseful.

ART DALEY: He hated to share the spotlight with anybody, which is human, I guess. I publish the Green Bay Packer yearbook and Vince was quite happy with it – "as long as you don't say anything foolish in it." I planned the 1965 yearbook with Tom Moore on the cover. Moore had a good year in '64 replacing Paul Hornung. Then something happened. Curly Lambeau, founder and coach of the club for 30 years, died on June 1, giving me barely enough time to get a big spread on him in the book – since it was due out July 20. I had shot a color picture of Curly and Vince in 1961 when Curly was elected into the Hall of Fame. It had been a struggle to get that picture, which was taken on a Saturday morning after practice in the stadium. Vince had been reluctant to have his picture taken. Well, I used this picture on the cover of the 1965 yearbook and he was furious. This explained why he didn't want that picture taken in '61. He just didn't want to share the spotlight with anybody, much less Lambeau, who really was kind of a saint in Green Bay. I sent 100 yearbooks to the Packer office in July and he blew his stack again, saying it was the worst book I ever produced. He slammed the phone down on me and he never actually spoke directly to me again until Oct. 29, 1965 – two days before our seventh game of the year. On that historic morning he called me at 9 o'clock and told me to come out to practice. So I came on the sidelines and he rushed over and extended his hand. "You're too nice a guy," he said. "I can't go on being mad at you." The players were flabbergasted.

JIM KENSIL: They were leaving Detroit from Willow Run in '65 and I was leaving from Metropolitan but he was in some kind of euphoric mood and he said, "C'mon. We'll drop you off." So I sat next to him on the bus. It'd been quite a game. The Lions had killed the Packers in the first half – they led 21-3 – but the Packers had gotten four touchdowns in the second half and won 31-21. I asked him what the hell he'd said at halftime and he laughed and said, "Sometimes you get lucky." He said that just before the half ended Alex Karras walked by the Green Bay bench and cursed at him. The players heard it and he didn't let them forget it. He said, "I told Kramer I wanted him to take care of that son of a bitch and I reminded the rest of the team of it, too." He was delighted to tell the story.

The bus had to make a detour to drop me off and it must have delayed the Packers about 15 minutes. The players were anxious to get to the plane, where they had beer waiting, so Lombardi stood up and said, "Don't blame me for holding you up. Blame this one on the league office." God, he was happy.

MEL DURSLAG: He snapped at me twice after a victory over the Rams and then I asked him, "How do you feel after you lose?" He smiled and said, "Probably a lot better." And then he said, "I'm sorry. I get touchy when my stomach gets upset."

LEAH LEVITAS: A win over the 49ers in 1965 would have clinched the title but it ended up in a tie and the

Packers were forced into a playoff with Baltimore the next week. So we had to forget our plans for a celebration that night. We waited around the bus anyway, with Marie, although I knew it was a mistake. When he came out he had his head down and I mumbled something — "Goodbye, Vince," I think — and he let out such a sigh of frustration you wouldn't have believed it. The next day he didn't remember having seen us after the game.

JOHN THOMPSON: I heard him give a speech once — after the '65 season. There was a big football banquet in Minneapolis and Lombardi was Coach of the Year and they asked him over to speak. He wasn't the featured speaker, though. Tom Harmon was. I'll tell you, Lombardi just gave a tremendous speech. He talked about competitiveness and the will to succeed and he compared football to life. He had the audience eating out of his hands — such emotion! Six years later you ask anybody who was there if they ever heard a speech like that and I'll guarantee you they haven't. Poor Tom Harmon! He had to follow all this and everything the poor son of a gun tried to say Lombardi had said a few minutes earlier in a much greater way. Just wiped him out.

DICK BOURGUIGNON: When the Atlanta Falcons started, Rankin Smith offered him a piece of the club. I put in a call for Vince when I heard that but with our busy schedules we always were missing each other. So finally I came down here on a Saturday and after practice I went up to his office. He asked me why I had been calling him. I said, "First of all I want you to know that I've heard from some pretty good sources that Smith has offered you a percentage of the Atlanta ball club and that you are considering it." He said, "Yes, that's true," and I said, "Well, I want to tell you something: I'm sure this is what you've always wanted — the ownerships part of it — and any help that I can give I will be happy to give. I won't stand in your way like I did when you wanted to leave and go back to New York. I'm going to tell you one other thing, too: You are going to be part owner but you are never going to be closer to actually owning a ball club than you are right here, in this setup. You are never going to find a group of people to work for like you have here." And he said, "Are you finished?," and I nodded and he said, "I want you to know first. I want you to know that I have notified Rankin Smith that I'm not interested."

JERRY ATKINSON: New franchises always looked in his

direction. But we had taken care of Lombardi from a financial standpoint — like nobody else was being taken care of in football.

NORB HECKER: After I took the Atlanta job I said that the one game I'd like to win that first year was with the Packers and Coach said to a reporter, "That was Norb's first mistake as head coach. It won't take him long to learn that a head coach had better keep his mouth shut." They beat us that first year 56-3.

JERRY BURNS: There was no small talk. No bartering. When he hired me he wouldn't play any games on salary. Instead of saying, "I don't know what you made at Iowa, but —" you know, the standard routine — he said, "What did you make at Iowa?" I told him. He said, "Here's what I can give." It was very fair.

¶ So he showed me around the Packer offices that day and I was very impressed. I said to him, "This building is a marvel. Its only purpose is football!" Those were my exact words. God, he just stood there with his hands folded in front of him, smiling and glowing. I think I said the right thing.

CHUCK LANE: I mentioned to him that there was a problem with the plumbing system in the visitors' locker room. The Bears were here and the Packers apparently got to the showers first. So when the Bears got there, there was no hot water left, absolutely none. We had just beaten them — beaten them badly — and then they got cold showers on top of it. They were really upset. I went in and just happened to mention it to him that day and he said he didn't give a damn, that the visiting team didn't matter anyhow.

MIKE MANUCHE: He said that he needed a certain type of football player. He said, "I know a lot of great players that I cut not because they couldn't play football but because they weren't made for my system." He said it was as simple as that. He said if you have a system, it's like you don't put spinach in a lemon cake.

¶ One time he said, "I'd rather have a player with 50% ability and 100% desire because the guy with 100% desire you *know* is going to play every day so you can make a system to fit into what he can do. The other kind of guy — the guy with 100% ability and 50% desire — can screw up your whole system because one day he'll be out there waltzing around."

PAT PEPPLER: He'd say, "You get me size, speed, quickness and ability — the best you can — and I'll get it out of him or I'll send him home."

¶ In one draft he says, "Let's find someone with

speed" – it was just before our turn to draft in the second round – and I said there's this guy here, Travis Williams, he's 210 and does the 100 in 9.4. And he smiles and says, "You don't have to do any more selling."

¶ He wasn't too big to change his mind. We took Lloyd Voss from Nebraska in the first round and Voss was just too tight, too tense, around here. He had no confidence. Then we switched him from defensive tackle to offense and Lombardi realized that Voss was not going to play here. He told me, "You'd better get what you can get for him." He had been high on Voss, too.

¶ He was really mad at us the year we took Donny Anderson. He wanted to trade that first pick to the Giants for a receiver – a guy most of us didn't like – and Don Chandler. We talked him into keeping our choice and taking Anderson.

BOB SKORONSKI: Some teams always gave us a hard time. It was Minnesota in those days. They had losing records then but they always gave us trouble. We always seemed to have Cleveland's number. We never lost to them.

ART ROONEY: He had such complete concentration during the season that, at times, he might have seemed a little abrupt. There was a reason for everything, though, and once, on a coast-to-coast flight, he talked about how lucky you must be to win a title. Like a golfer who remembers each shot, Lombardi remembered all the breaks of the season that went in his favor, fumbles recovered, punts that rolled out of bounds instead of into the end zone.

RAY BILOTTI: After one of the championship games – I forget which one it was – he was going to come to our place with his party. The place was quite packed at the time and so we passed the word to a few friends – close friends – that when he does come in let's give him a nice hand. We didn't tell many people. When he did come in, the whole place got up, every person in the dining room, every one of them, stood and applauded and yelled for five minutes. God, I get goosebumps just thinking of it!

CHUCK LANE: He knew where every paper clip was. That's the kind of control he kept – from top to bottom. A lot of times I thought all these details really had to clutter his thinking. But that's the way he wanted it. He insisted on control of everything. Even my releases. He'd check them over and make changes. After a while I knew what to write. Like you didn't *whip* the Atlanta Falcons 56-3. You didn't *clobber* the Atlanta Falcons 56-3. You just *defeated* the Atlanta

Falcons 56-3. He didn't want to give an opponent anything that might make them play harder next time. He read and reread those releases, just like he was grading an English paper.

ROBERT LIPSYTE: I asked Lombardi, "What about this problem of not enough competition, what Kramer said." And Lombardi said, "Kramer who?," and I said, "Your guard." Lombardi said, "He didn't say that," and I said, "But I heard him on the radio," and Lombardi said, "Don't come in here and tell me things like that."

BOB SKORONSKI: It's really amazing the way he controlled. You had 20 guys going to banquets and every guy said the same thing. And he never told them what to say! You'd go someplace and they would say that there was no sense getting a Packer for the banquet because they all say the same thing anyhow. And are you aware that he actually controlled the press, too?

FATHER DAVID RONDOU: Of course everybody in Green Bay knew him. He could park his car in a no parking zone and nobody would bother him.

JIM KENSIL: We had a coaches' meeting on this ranch near Dallas and a photographer from *Sports Illustrated* wanted to get a picture. He had this idea that all the other coaches would sit on horses with lassos and Lombardi would be standing in the middle – the victim they all wanted to get. Vinnie wouldn't buy it and he was very obstinate. Rather than make a scene, I said nothing and I let them take a compromise picture. That night there was a cocktail party and he came up to me and said, "I don't ever want to be involved in a stunt like that again." He thought it would hurt his image. So we got in a shouting match that was a classic and he was steaming. A half hour after it was over he came back to me and said, "You know, you do a helluva job." I thought he was needling me but he really was sincere. For the next 20 minutes he went on to say nothing but nice things. I learned that day that the best way to get along with him was to argue and fight right back. He liked that.

¶ There were a lot of times when we'd argue back and forth about this and that and then he'd say, "Do I really have anything to say about this?," and I'd say, "No," and he'd say, "All right – but I don't like it." And that would be it.

PETE ROZELLE: Respect wasn't a one-way street with him. He demanded it of others but he also gave it. He gave it to me.

JIM LAWLOR: One night we were walking across the St. Norbert campus and he put his arm around my shoulder and said, "I wish this was the old days and you and I could ease off campus and go for a few brews." I said, "Great! Why don't we?," and he said, "Any place I go somebody wants to fight me." He said, "I got knocked on my ass not more than two weeks ago. Tom Miller and I were coming from some place in northern Wisconsin and we stopped for a beer. It was a hot day and I'm halfway through my beer sitting on the stool and some drunk walks up and punches me right in the mouth and says, 'I just wanted to see how tough you were.' "

PAT PEPPLER: He had the ability to look at a guy and say, "That's the kind of guy that could help me win a championship." Not just a good football player, not even, necessarily, an All-Pro performer. I think a perfect example is Ben Wilson. He paid a pretty high price for Ben Wilson – a second-round draft choice – but he got one year of football out of him, far more than anybody else would have gotten out of him. And he won the third championship with him. When Taylor left us Vince came to me and he said, "Well, we need another fullback. I've got to have another one." And so in came Ben Wilson, all rubber-legged. He couldn't run a 10-yard sprint – or run on a straight line. He wobbled all over the place. I know he told me after about a week and a half, he said, "I've never been worked so hard in all my life. In Los Angeles we used to play golf between workouts. Here you go to bed."

BEN WILSON: Coach told me I was dropping too many passes. He said to go see an eye doctor. So I did and the doctor said he was surprised I had *ever* caught a football with those eyes of mine.

DICK BOURGUIGNON: As far as three people are concerned, Tony Canadeo and I enjoyed something with that man that no one else in Green Bay ever had, really. I remember one time, during his last year of coaching here, when we were down there discussing something and it ended up that we didn't quite agree with him and so we were arguing. And Tony said, "Look, you had better knock that crap off right now." And Vince kind of looked back at Tony and said, "What do you mean?," and Tony said, "You keep up that kind of attack and you're going to lose your two 'yes' votes!" Vince laughed like hell.

¶ We didn't always agree with him. But most of the time what he had to say was pretty damn solid.

When we didn't agree, we'd have to sit down and discuss it and hack it out and he'd say, "Gee, I didn't think of that." Or sometimes he'd say, "That's a better idea."

PAT SUMMERALL: We were sitting around Mike Manuche's one night, Vince and I, and Art Modell and Bill MacPhail, my boss at CBS, were there, too. It was after the second year they had played inter-league preseason games between the NFL and AFL. The first year the NFL won big, like 16 to 3. The second year they scheduled more of them and the AFL won like 16 to 13. We had a few drinks. MacPhail was talking, saying, "We're saying at CBS that we've got the best football there is. We're getting 60,000 bucks a minute. NBC is getting 16,000 bucks a minute, yet they're beating us 16 to 13. It's just a matter of time. How long are we going to be able to say, to convince them, that our product is superior to their football?" And the more we talked the madder he got because he felt that some of the teams were not going all out to justify the rights money we had paid. He got madder and madder. Finally I said to him, "Why don't you take it easy? You're getting excited and you're getting emotional about this damn thing. Don't get mad. It's no big thing. The regular season is coming up." And Lombardi turned on me and he said, "It *is* a big thing, mister. I'll never give a game to an AFL team and if you can't get emotional about what you believe in your heart then you're in the wrong business." He almost stuck his finger through my chest.

BOYD DOWLER: The 1961 and 1962 teams, I believe, were a cut above everyone else. But by 1965 and in the two years after that, too, things had evened out a lot. There were four or five other teams with comparable personnel. They could have won it. The point is they didn't. We won it and I know now it was the motivation the man gave us that did it.

BART STARR: He said, "They are going to remember you won it in '61 and '62 and '65 and '66 and '67 but they aren't going to know that you existed in '63 and '64. They don't ever remember who finished second. Only champions."

FUZZY THURSTON: The only victories we really could savor were the ones that were the last of their seasons. Every other win was just a prelude to the next big game.

TOM BROWN: Lombardi said no team would ever win three consecutive world championships again. He said the teams are too well balanced now.

JIM LAWLOR: Once on the sideline – in '67 – he asked me, "What do you think about me giving up the coaching job?," and I said, "I think it's a good idea. If you make it this year you've had your three champions and there's nothing else you can try for. Besides, you're not getting any younger" – he was 55 then, a year younger'n me – "and you're putting in too much time for a guy your age." And he said, "What the hell do you mean *a guy my age?*," and I said, "I'll be honest with you. I'm not afraid of you. You're getting old, same as I am. You're up at 6 o'clock in the morning and you hit the sack at maybe 12 o'clock at night and you're going all that time. Now, I don't give a damn who you are, you can't do that for long." He said, "Maybe it would be better if I did," and that's the last thing he said. A few weeks later he retired and it came out in the papers.

EDWARD BENNETT WILLIAMS: He was exhausted so instead of taking a nice long rest of eight or ten weeks and just getting away from football he said, very emotionally, "I'm gonna quit." And of course no sooner had he quit when he began to feel the first pangs of regret. The day he watched the Packers play from the pressbox for the first time he knew he had made a horrendous mistake.

CHUCK LANE: I think what really drove him out of the coaching business – temporarily – was the constant pressure. I don't think the guy could ever relax.

PAUL BROWN: One time he called me on the phone and he was upset because they were making him out to be a Mussolini or a Mafia man or something. They were creating an image of him, an image that he felt really hurt him. He was upset about it. He said, "What can you do about it?," and I said, "Vince, I'll tell you how I feel about it." I said, "I just think you ought to live with it and be yourself and the truth will eventually come out as to the kind of person you really are."

HOWARD COSELL: He was deeply affected by the image that was built up by the media. I believe that drove him out of coaching in Green Bay. When he came back he told me he wasn't going to let it affect him this time.

MIKE MANUCHE: He was very upset with the article that was written in Esquire. His mother called him up and said, "What kind of an article is this?," and he really got upset then. That was one of the reasons why he retired and left coaching that year.

¶ I would tell him, "There always are going to be

people who say bad things like that, who really don't know you. They don't know all the good things you do. They don't know the character you've developed. They see you yelling and screaming. They don't see you when you advise a young man what to do and how you help them." So he thought about it and he said, "You need those guys, too, because a lot of people want to read stuff like that. They don't want to read that you're a nice guy. They want to read that you're a bad guy. Some people see the good and some see the bad and you need both kinds."

COOPER ROLLOW: The piece in Esquire upset him more than usual. The writer detailed a conversation with a Green Bay waiter in which the waiter presumably was asked, "What is Vince Lombardi really like?" "I'll tell you what he's like," the waiter was quoted as replying. "If you can help him nothing is too good for you. But if you can't help him"– the waiter picked up a dinner knife from the table and flicked it across his throat. Lombardi turned purple when he read the passage. "Am I like this?," he yelled, hurling the magazine to the floor and slamming his fist on the desk. "Am I really like this?"

JERRY ATKINSON: He should never have worried about all the small stuff, about what time the bus was going to leave, stuff like that. But he insisted on it. He insisted on doing everything. I think that's part of what happened to him in the year he was out of coaching. He really began to believe that he wasn't needed, that he wasn't useful.

MAX MC GEE: After we were winning a lot, it was easier on the players but harder on him. And it got to the point where there was nothing more left for him to do in Green Bay. I mean, three titles in a row! Another thing was maybe that he wanted people to know he was the reason for our continued winning. I mean I loved the guy but you have to say he was very egotistical.

CHUCK LANE: When Phil Bengtson got the job I felt we should look for things to try to build Phil's reputation and why Lombardi had chosen him. So I proceeded to publicize the fact that Phil's defenses had never finished below second in comparative league statistics. I thought it would make Phil look better. The minute after that release was on his desk, Lombardi came through that door full speed. He reminded me – in no uncertain terms – that it wasn't *Phil Bengtson's* defenses it was *his* defenses and that Phil Bengtson was merely implementing or installing them.

BOYD DOWLER: After the '67 season I set a goal of X number of dollars for my contract. We'd just won three titles in a row and I thought I was coming off what was my best year. So I went in to him and I told him how much I wanted and he said, "I think you deserve that, too." Then he told me what a really great year I'd had and he had me feeling really good, really high. An hour later I walked out of his office with a signed contract in my pocket. It was for $4,000 less than I'd asked for. I don't know how he did it.

PAUL HORNUNG: He always was fair to me when it came to contracts but it still was a game. Once I agreed to terms on a golf course. Afterwards, we had a couple of drinks. So the next morning I go in to sign. It went like this – Him: "What did we talk about yesterday?" Me: "X dollars." Him, getting mad: "I would never agree to that much. Don't kid me." Me, getting madder: "You agreed yesterday." He smiled and he said that, yes, it was a fair price. He had the contract drawn up then but I never knew whether that whole scene was part of his game.

RAY BILOTTI: We talked about having a Lombardi Room for a long time, Duds and I, but to tell you the truth we were a little worried about how he'd react to it, I mean a special room with his name attached to it in a public restaurant. One day the opportunity came and when he was here for lunch we approached him and he almost had the attitude like, "How come you guys didn't ask me sooner?" He seemed to be real pleased about it.

¶ The night we opened the room we had a surprise party for him. All of his friends were there and he was living it up good. He was talking and laughing with everybody when he noticed our brother-in-law who he hadn't met and he walked across the room to him and said to him, "I don't think I've had the pleasure of meeting you," and introduced himself to our brother-in-law. He could be gregarious like that but the majority of times he'd just stand there and let them come to him. Mostly it was the mountain coming to Muhammad.

GEORGE HALAS: I enjoyed those off-season meetings with Vince – at banquets and league meetings. I remember making a speech at a testimonial banquet for Vince in Green Bay. I said I felt out of place at a testimonial, that I always came to Green Bay to bury Caesar, not to praise him. Vince liked that. Later he said he hadn't realized I was so erudite. I've been in pro football 50 years and that was the first time anyone accused me of being erudite.

DOM GENTILE: One time he wanted to go play golf on Friday and he called me on Monday. This was during the off-season. He said his back was killing him, absolutely killing him, and could I help him? So I came out and he was so stiff and sore and unable to move that I decided we should put some ice on it, anesthetize it a little bit so that we could get him to move it a little. So I had him lay down on the table. The moment I put that ice bag on his back he about jumped up and strangled me. But then he swore and suffered through that treatment and the next day, when he found out it was doing him some good, it was less painful for him.

JACK TEELE: I was in New York for the expansion meeting when New Orleans selected players and the day I was there Lombardi spoke to the National Association of Manufacturers. And here he is – and no matter what we say it was a football coach talking to millionaires and scions – telling them how to run their companies. The central theme was to be the boss. "Don't be afraid to be a leader," he said. "Men want to follow. It gives them security to know there is someone who cares enough to chew them out a little bit or to correct their mistakes." These leaders of industry, these millionaires, gave Lombardi a standing ovation.

BUD LEVITAS: The story about him being approached to run for governor of Wisconsin in 1968 was a true one. There was a lot about politics that appealed to him but he knew and I knew that he wasn't a compromisor. He told me he wasn't suited for that kind of game.

DOM GENTILE: During the presidential elections of 1968 most schools in the area had mock elections. Lombardi received a great many votes. During a discussion about this one time he told me that he had been approached to run for the U. S. Senate. He was very concerned about the lack of statesmen and the overabundance of politicians. But he said that wasn't a field for beginners.

ED BRESLIN: I encouraged him to go into politics but he said, "I don't like that hand shaking stuff." I said, "Listen, if you run for the Senate, I'll go around and shake hands for you. You just make the speeches." He had a great feel for everything that was going on in this country. He could talk to youth.

MARIE LOMBARDI: I hated to see him coach. I really did.

I hated to see him on the sidelines. When he came alive, really came alive, was when he was on a dais. The last few years he was an incredible public speaker. I heard the same speech – the same basic thoughts – over many times but every time I heard them it just knocked me off my feet.

OCKIE KRUEGER: I used to go on a lot of speaking engagements with him and initially I thought he was just throwing things out there for public consumption. So I said to him one day, "Oh, that horseradish that you put out," and he got very indignant about it and I realized that everything he was saying came from way down deep inside. All the things he said about the church and the family and football and youth, about football being a Spartan game. He meant them. He didn't convince me by talking to me but he did convince me by me listening to him talk to other people.

¶ It was like that sales film he did, "Second Effort." People in Milwaukee – these were big industrialists – would say, "This is the greatest thing in the world. The best thing I ever saw."

VINCE LOMBARDI, JR.: I saw the movie in Minneapolis and the next time I saw him I said, "When it comes to acting ability, Richard Burton and Paul Newman don't have too much to worry about." He laughed but then he got all huffed up and said, "Tell me what was wrong with it. Tell me."

DAVE SLATTERY: At a league meeting he said to me, "Now don't get excited but I'm going to put on a little performance to get this one across." He ended up getting 24 of the 26 team votes on that one.

JACK TEELE: He could fix you with that stare and that firm look of his and he'd make you think, hey, I'd better think over my no vote or my yes vote.

¶ At one meeting, someone said they were having labor negotiation problems and with the players you had to do this and you had to do that – putting down the players pretty good. And Lombardi leaped up and said, "Good God, man! Don't you realize that these men are artists – artists! You aren't dealing with a bunch of hodcarriers or truck drivers. These men are artists, skilled artists, dammit!" You know, you could just see the fire in him.

JIM KENSIL: He'd drive me crazy in meetings. It was either too hot or too cold. There was something wrong with the air conditioner or there was something wrong with the furnace.

"Right now we are engaged in a struggle that is far more fiercely contested than any football game. It is a struggle for the hearts, it's a struggle for the souls and it's a struggle for the minds of all of us. This is a game in which there are no spectators, only players. It's a struggle which is going to test all our courage, and it's a struggle which will test all our stamina. It's a struggle which will test all of our strength. And unless we're physically ready and mentally ready and spiritually ready, we may not win this big one."

MARK DUNCAN: I never really realized what a highly organized man he was until I spent two years with him on the Competition Committee. All his thoughts were organized. He didn't want to leave anything undone, any loophole. He wanted everything to be as perfect as he could make it.

¶ He didn't talk unless he had something to say and when he had something to say everybody listened.

JIM FINKS: We were together on the Player Association committee and in one session, one bitter session, a lawyer for the players named Shulman used some foul language. Lombardi knew it was a test of his image, of his strength. He replied, "Listen mister, if you want to play down in the gutter, then I'll play there, too," and he proceeded to rip this guy and what he had said for about 10 blistering minutes. He laughed about it that night and even though he had been serious earlier he said, "If that doesn't get me an Oscar, then nothing will!"

ARTHUR MODELL: Oh, this was a scene! Lou Spadia comes into a Players' Association committee meeting and Lombardi's in a bad mood and so he says, "Get the hell out of here. You don't belong here." Spadia didn't say a word and he went over in the corner and put his head down. So I said to Vince, "Hey, Vinnie, you can't do things like that. Especially not to a club owner," and Vinnie said, "You're right," and he went over in the corner and put his arm around Spadia and said something. A few minutes later they rejoined the rest of the group, laughing and joking.

MAX MC GEE: I pulled the bread and fish thing on him at the testimonial banquet they gave him before the '68 season. Just before the food was served – there were about four or five thousand people there – I brought out this platter and on it were five fishes, little ones, and nine loaves of bread. He just about rolled on the floor. It brought down the house.

JIM LAWLOR: In the last year in Green Bay two nuns came up to him and they wanted to know if they could purchase tickets to go to the intrasquad game and he said, "How many of you are there, sister?," and she said there were about 40 and he said, "I'll tell you what, sister, I'll see that the 40 of you get tickets providing that you come to our buffet and beer party after the game." She said, "We'll have to get permission from the Father," and he said, "Father who?," and she said, "That's him over there." Vince went over to him and came back and said, "Sister, the 40 of you will be my guests at the game and you will come to our beer party afterward."

MARIE LOMBARDI: He always felt guilty about not spending every moment on football. He felt guilty about playing golf. Once in the spring after he had resigned as coach – he's not even coaching any more now, understand – he came home in the afternoon with a funny look on his face. I said, "Did you play golf today?," and he said, "It snowed today." I said, "I didn't ask you if it snowed. I asked you if you played golf." He couldn't keep a straight face.

OCKIE KRUEGER: In the summer of the year he retired we played golf a few times and he would have a bad round and he'd say, without thinking, "I'm sure ready for camp."

JIM LAWLOR: I came into his office and we shook hands and I said, "I'm going out to practice." This was in 1968. And he said, "I wish I was, too."

¶ So I went to practice and I just happened to glance down the field and there he was, all by himself, down behind the goal posts watching. And as soon as practice was over I got in the car with him and I said, "You're eating your heart out, aren't you?,"and he said, "Yes, I'm eating my heart out."

CHUCK JOHNSON: He was lost on the sidelines in practice then and once Henry Jordan saw him standing there and said, "Coach, do you want to chew us out for old times' sake?"

WILLIE DAVIS: We missed him as much as he missed us. He'd come down to practice now and then but no one talked to him because if you did then that would indicate that you weren't totally concentrating. We spent that whole '68 season waiting for that voice to come rolling in, that "Do this!" voice that we had come to rely on. He spoke to the team a couple of times but it really wasn't the same. We needed him as Number One.

MORRIS SIEGEL: When he came to Washington in 1968 for a game against the Redskins, he was offered a seat in the box set aside for visiting owners. He declined and said, "In the first place I'm not an owner. And in the second place –" He pointed inside the box to Mrs. Lombardi and chuckled and then he told us how he never sat with his wife at a football game. "I annoy her," he said and then he chose an obscure seat in the pressbox.

ED BRESLIN: After the third game of the season he said to me, "This is killing me. I just can't stand it."

I told him not to worry. I told him to relax because the season had a way to go and maybe it would get better. He said, "I know me. It'll get worse." It did.

DICK BOURGUIGNON: There were many times during that season when he would just fight with himself to keep from going down and talking to the team. He would pace in that office of his and he would say, "I can't do it but I should. I can't do it." He felt that he had given Phil the job as head coach and it wouldn't be fair for him to interfere. That's why he *never* would have replaced Phil as head coach.

BUD LEVITAS: When he came to San Francisco for the game with the 49ers he was like a caged lion. He didn't know what to do with himself. Before the game that day I had my six-year-old grandson with me in the booth – the kid loves football – and Vinnie says to him, "Bobby, I've got one bit of advice for you. You just get ahold of a football and kick it and kick it and kick it. Kickers have got it made in this game. That's what'd interest me if I were starting over." I had to turn around and smile. He wasn't kidding me.

MARIE LOMBARDI: I didn't say much about his players around him. One time, though, when Vinnie was up in his little private cubicle in '68, Donny Anderson made a nice run and Vinnie said Anderson was going to be the greatest halfback in the history of pro football. Anderson had been around three years, I guess, and he'd never shown promise of that so I said, "Quiet. You sound like you're crazy." Ooh, did he jump back at me for that one.

TONY CANADEO: He just had to go back to coaching again. He felt lost up in that pressbox. He was the type of general who couldn't fight a war from his desk. He had to be down on the field with us, with his people, yelling, "What the hell is going on out there?" That was it right there – "What the hell is going on out there?" You could hear him up in the pressbox.

OCKIE KRUEGER: We were in a hotel room and he was talking to the owner of another ball club on the phone. I knew there was some kind of deal in the wind because he was very nervous. He weighed one thing and he weighed another and he talked about being offered stock in this club – which is the only way he could have left Green Bay. He went into the other room of the suite and he was not gone too long before he came back and said, "I just turned down a million bucks." And he laughed, kind of a serious, half-sick laugh. He said how happy he was and how he never could go to another place. Of course the million dollars was in stock, not small unmarked one dollar bills.

TONY CANADEO: He had chances to leave for New York and we said no. More than one time. The Rams wanted him. I'm sure he could have had the Atlanta job . . . the New Orleans job . . . the Philadelphia job. Let's face it, they just wanted the best man.

HOWARD COSELL: I was commissioned by Sonny Werblin to ask Lombardi to come to New York to meet him, to discuss taking over the Jets. I called Vince in Green Bay and he said, "Howard, I would love to do it but I can't do that to the Maras." I said, "Vince, this could be your final fulfillment as a coach. To coach that boy. To coach Namath." He said he couldn't. Loyalty.

MAL FLORENCE: He always returned my phone calls. When George Allen was fired for the first time by Dan Reeves in December of '68, it was no secret that the Rams tried to hire Vince. Reeves even met with him in Los Angeles. I was aware of this and tried to call Vince in Green Bay. His answering service said he was in Miami but they wouldn't tell me where he was staying. I left my name and number. Two weeks later Allen was rehired and I forgot about my call to Lombardi. Then, while I was attending a Pro Bowl luncheon at the Biltmore, I was paged. It was a long-distance phone call from Lombardi, who had tracked me down through my wife. He said, "I'm returning your call, Mal. What do you want?" I sputtered around and then I remembered my original intent. I told him I had called — two weeks earlier — to ask if he were interested in the Ram job. Vince laughed and said, "I think that's a little after the fact now, don't you?"

DOMINIC OLEJNICZAK: He had a chance to get a piece of an oil well if he went to Los Angeles.

DICK BOURGUIGNON: The fall before he left I remember we played the Redskins in Washington and I was on that trip and on Saturday night I went out for dinner with Vince and Marie. And that was the night that he told me that he'd gotten an offer from the Redskins and that he was seriously considering it. He asked me what I thought and I told him, "Well, you've always wanted a piece of a ball club. That always has been your ambition and I can't blame you for it. And I said as far as I'm concerned you can go with my blessing." He thanked me for it and said he was going to look into it. So one night after that he called me at home about 9 or 9:30 and he asked me what I was doing and I said I was reading the paper. He said, "Why don't you and Lois come over to the house. I want to talk to you," and I said, "I don't think I want to hear what you have to tell me." He started to cry over the phone.

LEAH LEVITAS: On the day he took the Redskins' job, the four of us — Bud and I and Marie and Vince — went out to the Racquet Club to celebrate. Vince and I were dancing and some guy edges up alongside us and say, "Congratulations," and Vince liked that. Then the guy says, "I'm from Chicago so take it easy on our Bears." That just made Vince furious. He said, "I hate it when anyone tells me that."

DUDS BILOTTI: After he took the Washington job we were sitting around drinking coffee and I asked him why he had done it. He took off his glasses and proceeded to tell us that he had made many mistakes in his life — many mistakes most people didn't realize — and one of them was quitting coaching. He said, "I was going bananas. I had to get back in it." He said he could have come back here but that would have meant hurting Phil Bengtson.

JIMMY CANNON: I know it was legal to leave Green Bay to go to Washington to get a piece of the club. I know he wanted that. I know that Green Bay is a tough place to live. But they *did* give him his opportunity. They *did* bring him out there. And because he stressed ethics and devotion and loyalty to one's principles, he offended me when he left for Washington. Somehow, I demanded more from him.

CHUCK JOHNSON: He was the speaker at the first Wisconsin pro football writers' dinner. It was just before he was to leave for Washington so it was his last public appearance in Green Bay. I had a copy of "Run to Daylight" and I'd been meaning for years to bring it around to have him autograph it. I took it along that night. And he wrote in the book: "With fondest memories. From a pauper in my field to a prince in his — Vince Lombardi."

CHUCK LANE: The day he left Green Bay he asked me to drive him to the club to pick up some of his equipment and then take him to the airport. That was really the first time that I had much of an opportunity to actually sit down and discuss various things with him. I wish the opportunity had come up much earlier than that.

EDWARD BENNETT WILLIAMS: It was a fact that he wanted to get out of Green Bay. Green Bay gave him his opportunity and he had a great debt of gratitude to the club and to the town but he belonged in the East. He loved the East. He was a New Yorker at heart and he longed for the day when he could come back East. This was an ideal setting for him because we were a rundown ball club in a great city and it was a tremendous challenge for him.

¶ I was at Senator Tidings' house for lunch one day right after Vince came here. It was a lunch that he was giving for Earl Warren, just after he left the Supreme Court, and the attorney general was there, John Mitchell, and he and I were talking about Vince. They had gone to Fordham at almost the same time and Mitchell said to me, "You know, when we were thinking of vice-presidential candidates in 1968 he was one of the persons we considered, but his political credentials were wrong." It was amazing but it was true. They not only had thought about him but they had thought of him fairly seriously.

OCKIE KRUEGER: He was the same in politics as he was in a lot of things. He always wanted the opportunity to say "no" but I really don't think he was interested. Like on the vice-presidential thing. They *did* call him. They didn't offer it to him but they asked him if he'd consider it.

FATHER TIMOTHY MOORE: I was around at Carlisle the day three kids quit. "If you quit now," he told them, "you're going to quit in everything you do in life. You're going to quit on life." He gave them a good lecture. That night he told me that he had planned to cut two of the three anyway but that was not a reason for giving up. He said, "They loved this game a week ago and now they don't. Meanwhile they all took their bonus money. This is an example of the moral code of our country. This is what our colleges are turning out now."

JOE BLAIR: He never liked to leave early because of the traffic. He always liked to wait until about 6 or 6:15. So a lot of times he'd just stop by my desk and we'd just sit there and chat. We talked football, about his players, about what happened that day.

TOM BROWN: Bobby Mitchell had worn a mustache for years and so had Charley Taylor. I wondered what would happen when they confronted Lombardi for the first time. You know, he never said a word about it to either of those guys. I don't know why. Maybe he thought that it was accepted now.

EDWARD BENNETT WILLIAMS: He was really fidgety before his first exhibition game with us and I told him, "It's only an exhibition. Take it easy. I saw some of your Packer exhibitions and you'd always play most of your rinky-dinks regardless of who you were playing." And he said, "I know, I know. I was an established coach then but I'm not now."

SAM HUFF: We played Pittsburgh and we beat them, like 14-10 or 14-7 or so. But we hadn't moved the ball well and he was miffed. At the start of the Wednesday practice one of the guys – I forget who – came out limping. He had a sore ankle and you could see it hurt. Lombardi turned on this guy and he said, "And what the hell's wrong with you?," and the guy said, "Bad ankle, coach," and Lombardi said, "I'll tell you this, mister, you're going to play Sunday if we have to carry you out there on a stretcher. Now run!" The guy did.

DICK BOURGUIGNON: It got to the point that last year in Washington, he would black out on the sidelines. And his own doctors told him to take it easy. *We* told him that. He wouldn't slow down.

BOB LONG: I had a terrible time with my back and legs and my elbow was just about shot. After every game I had a sack of blood on the elbow and it had to be removed. The pain was awful. Coach was gentle and understanding. It was like he knew what it was like.

LEAH LEVITAS: On the Sunday night of the Redskins' game with New York he had a big grin on his face. "I asked the team to win this one for me," he said. "I told 'em I'd never ask 'em this favor again." Then he laughed loud and said, "But I will!"

EDWARD BENNETT WILLIAMS: When he came here he had nothing like the personnel he had in Green Bay and so he drove himself harder than perhaps he ever drove himself. He did a fantastic job. He may have done his greatest coaching job in 1969. If there were some way to measure what one can do with the material at hand, I think we could demonstrate he did his greatest job here. He turned it all around, from going downhill to starting it back up. And, of course, once he died that was all lost. The momentum was lost. And then it just reverted back to what it had been.

DICK BOURGUIGNON: Vince came back to Green Bay last May for the first time since leaving and as a gag Circuit Court Judge Bob Parins bought a set of mutton-chop sideburns which he wore that day. When they shook hands Vince laughed and said, "Get a shave!" The judge removed the sideburns and Vince chuckled and said, "Let me have 'em. I'll wear 'em on the first day in training camp. If I see some of our players with long sideburns I'll yank mine off and say, 'This is what to do with these things.'" He never got to carry out his gag.

CHUCK LANE: This may sound goofy but when he came back here to visit that last spring, the tempo of the office picked up 300%. Now at that point he couldn't have fired anybody. He couldn't even have shouted at anybody. But the tempo picked up because he was coming out there. I didn't want him to come in here and see a messy looking office because he was always giving me a hard time about that. The girls in the office didn't want to have their hair messed up. They snapped to it. The whole efficiency of the place picked up. You wouldn't have believed it.

ART DALEY: He returned to Green Bay for a few rounds of golf in the spring. After a bull session I said flat out, "Why the hell don't you come back to Green Bay? This is where you belong." Those big brown eyes welled up – I thought he was going to cry, I did – and he only said, "I can't."

DICK BOURGUIGNON: He would just sit there and cry about it, about going to Washington, and he would say it was the worst mistake he ever made.

"I never could see any reason why we should lose."

Games

"We never won as many as I wanted—which was all of them."

THE TEN SEASONS

Year	Preseason Games			League Games			Post Season Games			Finish
	W	L	T	W	L	T	W	L	T	
1959	4	2	0	7	5	0	0	0	0	Third in Western Conference
1960	6	0	0	8	4	0	0	1	0	Western Conference Champion
1961	5	0	0	11	3	0	1	0	0	NFL Championship
1962	6	0	0	13	1	0	1	0	0	NFL Championship
1963	5	1	0	11	2	1	1	0	0	Second in Western Conference
1964	3	2	0	8	5	1	0	1	0	Second in Western Conference
1965	4	1	0	10	3	1	2	0	0	NFL Championship
1966	3	2	0	12	2	0	2	0	0	NFL & World Championship
1967	6	0	0	9	4	1	3	0	0	NFL & World Championship
1969	2	4	0	7	5	2	0	0	0	Second in Capitol Division, Eastern Conference
Totals	**44**	**12**	**0**	**96**	**34**	**6**	**10**	**2**	**0**	

1959-67, Green Bay Packers; 1969, Washington Redskins.

"When you win you get a feeling of exhilaration. When you lose you get a feeling of resolution. You resolve never to lose again."

Games: the memorable ones

He coached the Green Bay Packers for nine seasons and the Washington Redskins for one and in that time there were 204 games.

It is difficult to distill the memories, the memories that included six Western Conference championships, five National Football League championships, two Super Bowl championships.

In 10 seasons, Vince Lombardi's teams finished first six times, second three times and third once (in his initial season in Green Bay). In 10 seasons, winning was indeed the only thing.

Fourteen games show how it was, from that first game against the Bears through the second improbable Super Bowl championship.

Seven of the games fall in the 13 months from January of 1967 to January of 1968. It was a year of theatrics that raised Vince Lombardi's name one notch higher. From merely extraordinary to simply unbelievable.

Fourteen games. Twelve of them victories. Two of them losses.

12-2.

A typical Lombardi season.

September 27, 1959

It's a funny thing, retrospect.

In the beginning, in 1959. Vince Lombardi wanted a five-year contract because he said he might not win a game for five years and who would want him then? He said winning takes time.

Sure. So does snapping your fingers.

In Game One, Year One of the football era that carries the name of Lombardi, the Packers swept aside their oldest rivals, the Chicago Bears and George Halas, by a score of 9-6.

The business of second efforts (and third efforts and fourth efforts) began that day, too. The Bears led 6-0 in the final quarter when a second-year fullback from LSU scored a touchdown and a third-year halfback from Notre Dame kicked the extra point.

That is how life under Lombardi began for Jim Taylor and Paul Hornung.

Not a whimper but with a bang.

VERNON BIEVER: After his first win, the fans rushed on the field to just touch him.

BILL FORESTER: He ended the speech before the game by yelling, "Now go through that door and bring back a victory!" I jumped up and hit my arm on my locker. It was the worst injury I had all year.

EMLEN TUNNELL: I knew right away in that first game we were gonna be good. Not great, maybe, but good. We played tough and Green Bay teams had never played tough. They gave up. This team didn't give up. We won it in the fourth quarter and afterwards we gave him a little victory ride. In the locker room he was proud, oh, was he! He said, "Well, we're on our way now!"

JERRY ATKINSON: The first game was against the Bears and after it was over and we'd won I went back to my apartment to call him. I wasn't sure he'd be home. I could hear some voices and laughing and I said, "Well, coach, you did it. Congratulations!" And he said, "Jerry, where the hell are you?" I said, "I'm at my apartment," and he said, "How come you're not out here?," and I said, "Was I supposed to be?" He said, "Well, I just thought you *would* be here. Listen, I haven't got time to ask. You always are welcome here on Sunday nights if you can come." And so we were together on all those Sunday nights for all those years.

December 26, 1960

They came together nine yards from the goal line, the one's arms wrapped around the other's shoulders. Chuck Bednarik squeezed hard on Jim Taylor and they fell together into the mud.

One got up a winner. The other got up a loser.

And Vince Lombardi burned.

In the championship game of the National Football League, the Packers' most notable opponents were the clock and the Philadelphia Eagles. In that order.

The Packers were long on first downs (22-13), total yardage (401-206), passes completed (21-9), plays from scrimmage (77-48) and turnovers (1-3).

They were short on time remaining (0:00) and points (13-17).

It was a day on which the Packers had trouble finishing what they started. Two first-half drives ended with three points not seven points and there were errors of omission and commission later.

Still, the Packers held a 13-10 lead over the Eagles and their crafty quarterback, Norm Van Brocklin, with less than a quarter remaining.

The touchdown that put Green Bay ahead—a five-yard pass from Bart Starr to Max McGee—was followed by a 58-yard kickoff return by Ted Dean. The running back finished what he started eight plays later when he scored from the 5.

The Packers had one last gasp, one final rush of adrenalin and anger.

The Eagles had Chuck Bednarik.

RED COCHRAN: We'd been spending all our time getting ready for the Eagles and now, here it was, just a couple days before Christmas and I hadn't done any shopping. I asked him if maybe I could get away at 8:30 one night to give me an hour of shopping time. He said, "Red, do you want to be Santa Claus or do you want to be a football coach? You can't be both."

JERRY ATKINSON: We had to spend Christmas Eve in Philadelphia, in that hotel, and he was greatly concerned about the boys being away from their families. He arranged for presents then and that night the team was in his suite opening gifts.

BOB SKORONSKI: He had warned us. He said, "You know we haven't got a thing really won yet until we win in Philadelphia." And we actually got beat. And it proved what he'd said. You see, nobody remembers the Packers of 1960; they remember the Eagles. They forget us. We found out that day. We never lost another playoff game.

JIM RINGO: We all shed our tears, naturally, and he said finally, "We are men and we will never let this happen again. We will never be defeated in a championship game again." He said, "Now we can start preparing for next year." And that's what we went home to do. To prepare. We came again in 1961, prepared. We knew, we felt inside our bodies that we were going to be champions, and we worked hard and our reward came.

BILL AUSTIN: Really, he never talked very much about any of the championship games or anything like that. He talked instead about the games we lost. Like the Eagles' game in 1960. That really galled him. He wanted to make sure we wouldn't lose like that again.

CHUCK BEDNARIK: After I tackled Taylor he didn't move for half a second and so I said to him, "Get up! This goddamn game is over."

I remember walking off the field with those guys and you know the kinds of things you say in a spot like that, like you offer consolation and you tell them they played a great game. That's just what I told those guys, Jimmy and Hornung. I told 'em they had a helluva team and that they'd be back in this game.

They were a strong team, physically great. And they executed even then. You could tell they had some kind of spark. Vince? In 1960 he was just another coach.

December 31, 1961

There are some who would tell you that the name of the game on a Dec. 31 in Green Bay is survival of the fittest.

The New York Giants would tell you that it is merely survival.

The score was 37-0 in Vince Lombardi's second championship game, a chilling display of power football.

It was 24-0 at halftime and the Giants' coach, Allie Sherman, didn't ever bother to use a blackboard. "What can you say?" he said later.

In the month of the Berlin crisis, three Packers played on weekend passes from Army Reserve units.

Paul Hornung scored 19 points and rushed for 89 yards.

Boyd Dowler caught three passes for 37 yards and one touchdown.

Ray Nitschke hounded Y. A. Tittle unmercifully. The quarterback completed 10 passes, six of them to the Giants.

It was the day, too, when Bart Starr came of age as a quarterback. He passed for three touchdowns—one to Dowler and two to tight end Ron Kramer—and averaged 16.4 yards on 10 completions.

Oh, and it also was the day when people in Green Bay began answering the telephone with something besides, "Hello." They said, "Titletown, U.S.A."

ETHEL KENNEDY: During the Wisconsin primary in the spring of 1960, John Kennedy spoke in Green Bay. Vince and Marie came to see him and Vince said publicly, "I'm with you all the way." His endorsement could not but help the Kennedy chances in this key primary state. A grateful future President never forgot. Neither did the football coach of the Green Bay Packers.

¶ A year and a half later, Green Bay was up for the championship in a playoff game against the powerful New York Giants. It was in the middle of the Berlin crisis and Paul Hornung had been recalled as a member of the reserves. Vince called the White House and within 60 seconds he was speaking to the President. The coach mentioned that Hornung had been called up and would not be able to play against the Giants. The President instantly replied, "Paul Hornung isn't going to win the war on Sunday, but the football fans of this country deserve the two best teams on the field that day." Paul had one of his greatest days ever that day and Vince won his first NFL championship.

DICK BOURGUIGNON: There had never been a championship game in Green Bay. Always before that whenever Green Bay had won they would play in Milwaukee. The people in Green Bay resented it. Lombardi knew that. So in 1961 we were talking, the Executive Committee, and we talked about the Milwaukee situation and Vince said, "I've got news for you. If I win this thing this year, I want it in Green Bay." That was it, period. He wanted Green Bay to be recognized.

BILL FORESTER: The week before the game, my daughter was in the hospital with pneumonia so he and Marie invited my wife and our two boys, ages 7 and 9, over to eat Christmas dinner with them. My oldest son could never play football because of a physical defect but he asked Coach Lombardi to be sure and have Green Bay draft him in 1974, the year he'd finish college. I will never forget his reply: "Byron, the way they are passing out money now, by 1974 all you will have to do is sign a contract and you can retire from the bonus that you will get." A less thoughtful or educated person might have given my son an answer that could have offended him.

JOHN SYMANK: I had received an injury in the last conference game and I wasn't practicing during the week after the season ended. At that time, too, Paul Hornung was on active military duty because of the Berlin crisis but he received a leave to come back and play. I was in the whirlpool when the phone rang and it was a general from the Pentagon calling Coach Lombardi. Bud Jurgensen, our trainer, told the operator that the coach was on the practice field and couldn't be disturbed. The general told the operator he'd call back in 10 minutes. So Bud and I decided that we best get coach off the practice field and Bud went to get him. Coach came in the training room and he started to pace like a caged tiger, chain smoking and fussing about Hornung. The general called back about five minutes later and told coach that Paul had left his post without signing out and technically was AWOL. He wanted to know did coach know where Paul was or where he could be reached? Then the general said he would call back in 10 minutes. That's 10 minutes more of practice time coach woud miss. There was more pacing and more cursing of Paul for doing a foolish, stupid thing. Then he made this remark: "That damn Paul will end up getting me called back into the service." Several puffs on his cigarette later he stopped and said, "John, it wouldn't be too bad. At least I'd be a brigadier general and not a stupid private like Paul!" And he let out a big roar of laughter. The general called back then and he told coach that Paul had signed out but that he'd signed in the wrong place. Everything was okay. After hanging up, coach said, "I've missed 25 minutes of practice because of this. I should fine Hornung 50 bucks a minute. But damn him, I sure will be glad to see him. We need him to run that 49 option."

WELLINGTON MARA: He met us at the airport when we arrived, on the Saturday before the game, and he took us for dinner to this wonderful little restaurant in a small town that was a ways from Green Bay. I remember thinking to myself how relaxed he was, how much he'd changed. I found out a moment after that how much I'd misjudged. He stood up, signed the check he'd called for and said, "You can find your own way back to town." Then he left. It was like he was saying that the game officially began then. It was a helluva long cab ride.

DR. ANTHONY PISONE: He invited me to sit on the bench and so before the game I was in the clubhouse. I was in his office when Bart Starr came in and Bart was as nervous as a hen on a hot quilt. I was very uncomfortable in that situation and so I said, "I'll leave the room," and Vince said, "No, no! You can stay right here." So Vince put his arm around Starr and said, "I don't want you to do anything else today except what you've been doing all year. And I *know* you can do it." I sat right there and watched the tortured expression leave Bart's face. He left that room a different person.

WILLIE DAVIS: He built it up so the thing was you were defending the pride of Green Bay as much as you were the pride of the Packers. It was Big Ol' New York against Lil' Ol' Green Bay. And we knew how much it meant to him personally. He felt he had earned the right to be a head coach long before that so when it became a reality he wanted to leave no doubt. There was an incredible driving force behind him and it was so obvious before that Giant game. It was like he wanted the Giants wiped out. The score was 37-0 but it could have been 100-0.

"We had one year's experience in the playoffs. And we had a little poise, something we didn't have last year against the Eagles."

"For a championship game, this was as fine as any team could every play. It was a magnificent effort, a team effort, like it has been all year. I told the team that they were the greatest in the history of the NFL and I meant it."

JIM RINGO: One of his philosophies was to attack a man at his strengths and once they were vulnerable the weaker points would come more readily. That's the way we attacked as a *team*. If we came up against a Big Daddy Lipscomb, who was the premier defensive tackle at that time, we went after him. Hence, the rest of the Baltimore defense, the weaker part, became more of a friend to us. And it demoralized the opposition. It was the same when we played the Giants, like in the championship games. We went right after Sam Huff because Sam Huff was supposed to be the best linebacker around and going after him and defeating him underscored the weak points in their defense.

PAUL HORNUNG: He was very proud of us, I know, in 1961. In that season, Bart called audibles 45% of the time. In the entire year we missed only two – maybe three – of them. That's about as close to perfection as you can get and Vince loved that. That victory over the Giants kinda summed that whole year right up.

RED SMITH: That night in Vince's home – it was New Year's Eve – the coach was pouring drinks for friends and there was a great big grin pasted on his face that wouldn't come off. He kept looking across the room at the laughing Hornung and saying that this was a guy who could shake you off your trolley or lift you out of this world, a guy who probably was neither the greatest athlete nor the greatest football player in the world but who had that special ability to rise to the occasion and be the greatest of the great when the challenge was sternest. And that grin never did come off.

November 22, 1962

They had won six games in the preseason and 10 more in the regular season. There had been scores like 49-0 (twice), 48-21, 41-14, 38-7, and 31-13.

Playing the Packers was mostly a matter of firing (meekly) and falling back (quickly).

It was, that is, until Thanksgiving Day.

On a day on which millions watched television while the turkey roasted in the kitchen, Roger Brown and Joe Schmidt and Alex Karras took turns smothering Bart Starr.

It was the antithesis of the Packer season, a defeat of humiliation, a defeat in which the intensity was not measured by the final score.

It favored the Lions by 26-14 but it was 23-0 at halftime and 26-0 early in the third quarter and the Packers' only solace was touchdowns that came in the final minutes.

The Lions cut off the Packers' running game, checking Jim Taylor on three yards in the first half. In the end, Green Bay could manage an offensive total of just 132 yards.

"We just ran over them," said Brown, the 300-pound tackle. "We just stuck it to them. We wanted them to see stars."

On this day it was mostly a matter of a fallen Starr. The quarterback was sacked 11 times.

WILLIE DAVIS: He had the feeling we were letting pressure bother us. He could tell. Before the game he said, "The hell with an undefeated season. The hell with it. If it happens, it happens." He said, "You guys just aren't playing with the old abandon."

There *was* pressure. Winning can do that. And we always had to take everybody's best shot. And that was a year when everybody was laying for us, when everybody wanted a piece of that streak. I know the Lions then, they took a lot of pride in playing us. They gave us fits. That day they got us down to the canvas and they never let us back up.

He was a strong believer in man-for-man coverage in the secondary. He felt the zone defense left the middle open and he always used that Lions game to illustrate it. Gail Cogdill ran a split up the middle. He was open, right between two defenders, and each of them was waiting for the other to take him. Cogdill got an easy touchdown. Except for very isolated situations here and there, we never used a zone again.

He was very realistic after the game. He didn't blow up. He didn't seem upset. He just said the right things. He said, "The real glory is being knocked to your knees and then coming back. That's real glory. That's the essence of it." He said, "This is one game. *One* game. It's just a temporary loss of pride. Let it be an example to all of us: The Green Bay Packers are no better than anybody else when they aren't ready, when they play as individuals and not as one." He talked to a lot of us individually then. He talked to Fuzzy Thurston, who had lost his mother earlier in the week and who'd just gotten wiped out by Roger Brown. He talked to Bart Starr and Bart said later that what he told him was that what he did was to let himself get hurried and rushed out of his pattern of doing things. He talked to me and he said, "Willie, we're going to come back. I know we are. We just have to button up our pride and we will come back."

JIM RINGO: We came home for the team party and my youngest son was crying. I remember Vince carrying him around.

WILLIE DAVIS: That loss did more than remove the pressure. From that point on we never again got shook by losing. We didn't ever like it but we became more realistic about it. After that loss we went on to win four world championships.

"I take all the blame for that one. It was coaching stupidity."

December 30, 1962

The temperature in Yankee Stadium was 15 degrees above zero. It was more like 15 degrees above the toleration level of the human body.

There was a wind out of the north and its velocity was 40 miles an hour. The earth became concrete and the erosion of cleats turned it into swirling clouds of dust.

Vince Lombardi said later he had never in his life been colder. You can imagine how the New York Giants must have felt.

The score was 16-7, the second championship for Lombardi and the Packers, the climax to a season in which the team from Wisconsin played 21 games and won 20 of them.

The Giants were shut out in this game a year earlier and there was small consolation on this day. New York's only touchdown came on a blocked punt.

The offense that was built on Y. A. Tittle, Alex Webster, Frank Gifford, Phil King, Kyle Rote and Del Shofner came away empty handed again.

For the Packers, there was Jim Taylor, knocking men to the ground in a performance that went beyond mere courage. Taylor was rocked by linebacker Sam Huff early in the game and the intensity of the collision caused the fullback to bite into his tongue. Taylor swallowed blood for the rest of the game. The Giants swallowed only bitter pills. Huff said later that Taylor wasn't human, that no *man* could have taken that kind of punishment. When the game ended, Jim Taylor had carried the football 31 times and gained 85 yards. He had scored the Packers' only touchdown.

And then there was Jerry Kramer, the erudite guard who had handled the Packers' placekicking duties since the fifth game of the season, when Paul Hornung was injured.

Kramer attempted five field goals this day and he succeeded from 26 yards, from 9 yards, from 30 yards. The nine points were the margin of victory.

EARL BLAIK: We had dinner together at the Metropolitan Club on the night before the Packers played the Giants in New York, in '62. They were two hours of great tension and many doubts. He was so emotional about this game, about playing for a championship in New York, that it was tearing him apart. Suddenly, out of nowhere and for no reason he shouted, "We're going to win!" and then he stood up and almost bolted out, not saying good night or goodbye or anything.

JIM KENSIL: The game was on Sunday but the Packers didn't arrive until Friday afternoon. We had this big press conference all set up for him at 5 o'clock – a lot of people were there – and everyone was looking at their watches. There was no Lombardi. So I called him and I said, "We're all waiting for you. You'd better get over here quick." He said, "For what?," and when I told him he said that he hadn't been informed. He said he couldn't come, that he had promised his parents he'd go see them in Jersey. We argued back and forth and then the commissioner walked up and I told Vince, "Just a minute," and I gave the phone to Pete. Their conversation lasted about 10 seconds and when Pete hung up he said, "He's on his way."

¶ On Sunday when Vinnie was leaving the locker room, I said to him, "I know you didn't want to come over Friday but I appreciate the fact that you did." He said, "You gotta remember one thing: If you're going to exercise authority you've got to respect it."

OCKIE KRUEGER: I flew out with the team and I was with him the whole week. Every night I went out for dinner with the Lombardis and I said that so and so wanted me to sit with them at the game and he said, "Listen, I have to freeze on the sidelines. You can freeze there, too." So I said, "Okay." So nothing happened and we get on the bus that day, riding to Yankee Stadium and suddenly I thought that I don't have a ticket for this game. He's sitting in the front seat of the bus and I thought, well, I can just bull my way into the game. And he's sitting just looking straight ahead and we're buzzing through Manhattan on our way out to the game so I tapped him on the shoulder. He looked around at me and said, "What are you doing here?" And I started laughing and he said, "What the hell you laughing about?" I had made arrangements for the trip and I had been around him all week and he said, "What are you doing here?"

BOB SKORONSKI: He said, "We aren't going to leave this ball park until we beat them."

JIM TAYLOR: You look back and you know that you had nothing left – nothing – and yet you still continued to play. Like that Giant game. No one knows until they are faced with it just how much pain they can endure, how much suffering, how much effort they have left. The coach stepped in and pushed a player beyond that point. That's the way it was that day.

JIM RINGO: I had a nerve problem in my right arm. It was numb and I couldn't center the ball. I didn't think I could play. I didn't want to hurt the team by trying it. So he came to me and said, "We've come this far. You have to play." I did and when it was over I felt a better man for having done it.

"You must be tough to survive against the Detroit Lions and the Chicago Bears and we're going to have to get tougher to stay on top."

ED BRESLIN: I went down to the locker room afterwards and this friend of mine's at the clubhouse door and so he lets me slip through, past that great group of press, and there I am inside the door. The first thing I see – the first thing – is this big finger in my face and it's Vince and he says, "No one is allowed in this room until I say so." I says, "Vince, it's me, Eddie," and he kept waving that finger. He was so caught up in the emotion he didn't know who I was.

"A third championship? I'm not going to think about that for a while."

"That's the fifth or sixth time that question has been asked. I thought we were going to have a real good time in New York this time with all the newspapers here on strike!"

BILL FORESTER: After we won the championship in '62, we flew back to Green Bay. We were leaving early the next morning for Dallas and my wife and I wanted to stop by his house that night and see him before we left. He was having a party for some friends and we weren't invited but we thought it wouldn't hurt to intrude under the circumstances. We were warmly received and before we left he pulled me aside and said, "Bubba, it's never been done three years in a row." I didn't know at first what he was talking about and then I realized all he had on his mind was winning again next year. I thought to myself, can't this man have just one night to enjoy winning before thinking about next year? But this was the man. This was Lombardi.

December 26, 1965

In the history of the old-line National Football League, only two games ever required sudden-death overtimes.

Vince Lombardi was a coach in both of them.

He was with the New York Giants in 1958, the director of the offense in that memorable 23-17 loss to the Baltimore Colts in Yankee Stadium.

And he was with the Green Bay Packers in 1965, on a December afternoon of steel-gray skies. The opponent this time, too, was the Baltimore Colts.

Seven years before it had ended with Alan Ameche plunging across for a touchdown. Vince Lombardi was in tears then in what was to be his last game with the Giants before moving to Green Bay.

This time it was to end with Don Chandler kicking a 25-yard field goal and Vince Lombardi atop the shoulders of his players.

The 13-10 victory was more than just the Western Conference championship game of one season. It was, really, the prelude to three seasons in which challenges merely became mountains to be climbed because they were there.

The Colts began the game with a running back at quarterback. Tom Matte, the plays taped to his wrist, was a fill-in for the injured No. 1 and No. 2 men, John Unitas and Gary Cuozzo.

It was a seeming mismatch, Matte against Bart Starr, but the odds were shortened on the game's first play from scrimmage. Baltimore's Don Shinnick picked up a fumble and ran 25 yards for a touchdown. The last futile attempt at a tackle was made by Bart Starr. The shaken quarterback got up slowly and moved to the shelter of the sidelines. His ribs were aching and he was not to play again this day.

His replacement was Zeke Bratkowski, who had thrown the ball only 48 times in the 14 games of the Packers' regular season. He had completed 21.

Against the Colts, Bratkowski attempted 39 passes and completed 22. He compiled 248 yards. As a unit the Colts had 175.

Bratkowski's accomplishments are not reflected in the scoring summary. His long pass to Carroll Dale in the third quarter preceeded a one-yard plunge to a touchdown by Paul Hornung. His short passes to Bill Anderson and Boyd Dowler set up the tying field goal. His long pass to Dale in the overtime moved the ball into position for Chandler's winning field goal.

The kick came after 13 minutes and 39 seconds of tension and a large share of the crowd of more than 50,000 flowed onto the turf of Lambeau Field.

As if Vince Lombardi didn't have enough problems. Now he had to worry about the field being torn up.

The next game was only seven days away.

"It was football as it should be played, a tremendous hitting game. There is more satisfaction for the coach in winning a game like that, too. A 42-47 game like that one we had with them two weeks ago leaves a bad taste in your mouth. That's not good football."

ZEKE BRATKOWSKI: I was on the phones when Bart got hurt and Vince turned to me and I don't think he said a word or anything – except maybe, "Get in there," or something like that. I went in without any warmups, just went in cold. But I knew how it would be, how it had to be. How he wanted it. I prepared for every game as if I were going to play in it and of course most of the time I didn't. But he demanded you be ready. He demanded that I be ready to fill in for Bart or that Elijah Pitts be ready to fill in for Hornung . . . and right down the line. So when I said I went in cold, I really wasn't *that* cold.

¶ I really don't know about that disputed field goal. I mean Bart did the holding and I wasn't even on the field but we were able to study a lot of films of it later – even end-zone cameras. To this day I don't know whether it was good or off to the left. But I do think it was a good call.

¶ At the start of the overtime I remember he said, "Now make sure you don't make any mistakes." We didn't make any, either, but things sure got harrowing there when we were moving into position for the field goal inside the 20 and no one wanted to fumble. It was something.

DON WEISS: There was a lot of controversy about the field goal by Don Chandler that sent the game into overtime. Some people – the Colts, especially – thought the ball had been wide to the left. So after the season Tom Matte and Lombardi were at a banquet together and Matte presented Vince with a special award: Some goal posts with an extension that jogged far to the left.

January 2, 1966

They had not played in a championship game for two years.

They were spectators in 1963, when they lost only two games, both to the Chicago Bears, the eventual champions.

They were spectators, too, in 1964, when they lost two games by one point and another by three points.

And they almost were spectators in 1965.

Needing a victory in their final game of the season in San Francisco to clinch the Western Conference title the Packers were held to a 24-24 tie, a result that left an even more significant deadlock.

Both Green Bay and Baltimore finished with 10-3-1 records in the West and they played it off in Wisconsin.

So they came back to Green Bay on the following Sunday, the Packers and the Cleveland Browns, the winners in the East.

And this is the way it looked before they began:

Bart Starr had aching ribs. Jim Taylor had a muscle pull. Boyd Dowler had a bad ankle and two damaged ribs. And the Browns had Jim Brown, the most dynamic force in pro football.

There were five inches of snow in Green Bay on the night before and it took most of the morning to remove it. Then they played a football game.

It was a power struggle for 30 minutes and at halftime the score favored the Packers by 13-12. It was a power failure for the Browns in the second 30 minutes and at the finish the Packers were dominant, 23-12.

The damp field slowed down Jim Brown. He could manage only 50 yards.

It did not slow down Paul Hornung and Jim Taylor. Together, their total was 201 yards.

"I'm a pretty nice fellow usually. They build me up as a hard man but I'm not."

PAUL HORNUNG: During the game, I came back to the bench after scoring a touchdown and I said, "It's just like the good old days!" Lombardi took up the cry. He said, "Did you hear that?! It's just like the good old days! Just like the good old days!"

LIONEL ALDRIDGE: There was a sign in the locker room and I think we all knew it related to our mission, to Jim Brown and all. It said: "Pursuit is the shortest course to the ball carrier and arriving there in bad humor."

BOB SKORONSKI: Like in this game, when we went against Jimmy Brown, he told Nitschke, "Now this is all you've got to do. Don't watch anybody else. This is your guy." You know that pass that Brown dropped in the end zone? He had it in his hands but Nitschke was all over him, just hustling and hollering and screaming after him.

"We have a meeting scheduled tomorrow to talk about next year."

January 1, 1967

It was a match of quick draws. On the one hand, the three-time champions of Vince Lombardi. On the other, the expansionist upstarts from Texas.

The shoot-'em-up that resulted was a classic of its kind, a staggering display of offensive football that tried the hearts of all who saw it.

The two teams managed a combined 785 yards and 61 points and it ended with a nation on its feet and the Cowboys two yards away from the touchdown and extra point that would have tied it.

Green Bay never trailed on this memorable New Year's Day but the scores are worth retelling.

Five minutes after it began it was 14-0, one touchdown coming on a pass from Bart Starr to Elijah Pitts, the other coming when Mel Renfro fumbled the ensuing kickoff and Jim Grabowski ran it in for a touchdown

You would figure the Cowboys had been mortally wounded but you would figure wrong. It was merely a flesh wound. Drives climaxed by touchdown runs from Dan Reeves and Don Perkins resulted in a 14-14 tie as the first quarter ended.

After that it went like this:

Starr passed 51 yards to Carroll Dale for a touchdown but a field goal by Danny Villanueva cut the Packers' advantage to 21-17 at halftime.

The margin was one point moments after the start of the third quarter and it was then when the shaken Packers began to regroup. Starr passed 16 yards to Boyd Dowler for one touchdown and 23 yards to Max McGee for another.

The extra point after the last touchdown was blocked but with less than 10 minutes remaining there was seeming breathing room at 34-20. It was not the Cowboys who were out of breath, however.

Don Meredith passed 68 yards to Frank Clarke and it was, suddenly, 34-27. The Cowboys had momentum and when they got the ball back they moved ruthlessly through the Packers' defense.

They advanced to the Green Bay 2 but an offside penalty pushed them back. They were at the 2 again with 30 seconds left to play and Meredith rolled to his right. The rush came from linebacker Dave Robinson and Meredith threw wildly. Tom Brown, the Packers' free safety, intercepted and was engulfed by his teammates.

Vince Lombardi, the proud father, stood there smiling. Now he had four NFL championships. And a few more gray hairs.

"There are a great bunch of men on this team. I'm proud of them no matter what happens."

JERRY ATKINSON: I was having breakfast that morning with Jerry Kramer when Bart Starr dropped by and had a cup of coffee with us. Bart sat there awhile and then he looked at his watch and said, "My God, I've got to get to devotions."

BOB SKORONSKI: He changed our offense completely around. In our Red formation we always swept to the right. From the Brown formation we always went to the weak side. When we got to Dallas he changed it all around. We never went right from the Red. We always swept left and went outside the other way. It was completely backwards to what the Cowboys must have expected. They had no idea what we were doing to them.

MAX MC GEE: When we're leading 34-27 and Dallas has a first down on the 2, we're terrified. There's nothing we can do but pray. We haven't stopped the Cowboys all afternoon and we know they're going to score and the game is going into overtime. If that happens, we're dead. Dallas has momentum and we're emotionally exhausted. Then somebody in the Cowboy line jumps offside and we're saved. To me, we won that game because of Vince Lombardi. Lombardi discipline was the difference. Nobody who played for Lombardi would ever have jumped offside and cost the club a ball game or a championship. He wouldn't have permitted it.

January 15, 1967

The team that had dominated its league for six seasons dominated all of professional football on Super Sunday I.

It was a game for two quarters but it was no contest in the second half and Green Bay swept aside the Kansas City Chiefs with yawning ease, 35-10.

The Packers always had been known as "money players" but in this game the label was a literal one. Victory was worth $15,000.

It was the old league against the new in the Coliseum in Los Angeles and the motivation was pride.

The Packers stuttered in the first half and their lead was 14-10 at the break. It was different when they resumed. Willie Wood intercepted a pass by Len Dawson and ran it back 50 yards to the Kansas City 5. Elijah Pitts scored on the next play and the Chiefs were a broken team.

The day's most notable backbreaker was a man who was approaching his 35th birthday. Max McGee, relegated to the role of a substitute and summoned only when Boyd Dowler was injured, caught seven passes for 138 yards and two touchdowns.

Super Sunday I was a day on which the Kansas City Chiefs found out how the other half lives.

FORREST GREGG: We didn't know a thing in the world about Kansas City. We had never seen them play except on TV. And Vince came out and talked to us. Our first meeting. And he left no question in our minds that they had a great football team. He said, "You look at the size of the people they have and you look at the reputation they had before they got into pro football and then you watch them on film and you are going to be convinced that you are going to be playing a good football team." He scared us to death. He really did scare us.

JERRY BURNS: He was concerned with *everything*. During the week before the game in Los Angeles he made it a point to ask all the wives how their rooms were.

BUD LEA: In practice that week, Vince was relaxing at the 5 o'clock club one day reading a newspaper and looking at television. He turned around to the bar and asked for a refill and during that lull, Red Cochran, an assistant coach, turned off the television. Lombardi returned to his seat and screamed, "Who turned off my program?" Cochran jumped to his feet and turned the set on again. Vince was smiling again and watching a "Tom and Jerry" cartoon. That's the last time anyone tampered with Vince's television.

JIM KENSIL: He was really annoyed at the press conference the Friday before the game. He was testy and grumpy. It was the worst I ever saw him in a mass gathering.

JERRY ATKINSON: The night before the game Chuck Conners came in and Vince seemed to enjoy that. It was letting down time.

BOB SKORONSKI: He played the whole day up as prestige for the NFL. He said, "We've got something they have all been waiting for and talking about." He said we can't let our league down. It was almost patriotic.

FRANK GIFFORD: Before the game I had to do a live on-the-field interview with Vince. I don't think he wanted to do it but he agreed in advance. Still, I was worried he might not show. Well, a half hour before the start of the game he comes to me and asks if we could do the interview. I tell him we're not on for 15 minutes. He came back to me three times during those 15 minutes. When it finally was time to go on he was there again. And this really was incredible: During the five minutes or so I talked to him he held onto me and he was shaking like hell.

"It's the first time the game has been played. I think the game has to have a little tradition before you can tell what it means. I'm very proud to be in it but winning or losing is not going to be the beginning or end of the world."

ZEKE BRATKOWSKI: Bart hit third down after third down pass to Max McGee because they covered the strong side and Max was just standing there. Bart just threw and threw and threw to him. And that goes along with Coach Lombardi's theory. He demanded that you throw the ball. He didn't care. When the linebacker is inside and rolls in, you throw the ball. I mean he would be very loud—"Throw the ball!" He didn't care if it was third and one or what, just throw the ball because he knew your percentage was going to be high. He expected it to be high. He demanded it be high. And so the receivers knew. They were so schooled and experienced that when they saw the linebackers inside they expected the automatic. That's the way it was with McGee that day.

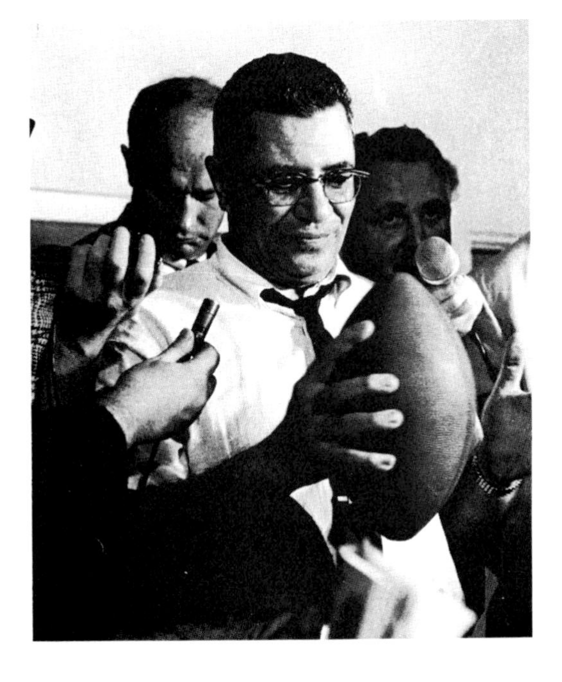

"The players gave me the game ball and I couldn't be prouder."

JIMMY CANNON: After the game, when the mass interviews were over, he gently pushed me into one of the cubicles they dress in in the Coliseum. He had a long-sleeved undershirt on and he had the game ball in his hands. We sat down in that cubicle and he talked about the things we both knew. But what I remember most of all is that he sat there with the ball and he patted it the way people pat cats and dogs. The football seemed to be a living thing.

JIM TAYLOR: My happiest memory of him is after we won that first Super Bowl out in Los Angeles. He was really pleased. That was the last game I played for him.

"The Chiefs are a good team but they don't compare with the top teams in the NFL. Dallas is a better team. That's what you wanted me to say, isn't it? Now I've said it."

OCKIE KRUEGER: They really forced him into the statement that the other league was not up to par and then he said, "You've been trying to get me to say it and now I've said it." He didn't want to say it, I know, but they just kept hammering and hammering. I was standing in the back of the room and I wanted to say, "Shut up!"

BUD LEVITAS: There had been so much tension before the game — you know, the old league against the new one — that, well, when it was over we were just jubilant. We brought the car around the Coliseum to where Vinnie would be coming out of the dressing room. When he came out, I could see he wasn't happy. He got in the car and I wondered if maybe we hadn't seen a different game. After a long period of silence he said, "I said something to the press and I wish I could get my words back. I told them that four of five NFL teams could have beaten Kansas City. It was the wrong thing to say, the wrong thing." We were driving up Wilshire Boulevard and he said, "I came off as an ungracious winner and it was lousy."

"Sure I think of quitting coaching. Every Tuesday after every Sunday I think of it."

November 12, 1967

The Germans have a word. Blitzkrieg. Lightning war.

Green Bay Packers 55, Cleveland Browns 7.

Zap! Pow! 55-7! Thud!

It began with an 87-yard touchdown run with the opening kickoff by Travis Williams, the now-you-see-him halfback, and it continued with a touchdown pass from Bart Starr to Marv Fleming and it continued with a touchdown run by Donny Anderson and a touchdown pass from Starr to Anderson.

Ernie Green gave the Browns a touchdown but Williams was there again, darting 85 yards through traffic to make it 35-7.

That was the way the first quarter ended!

What happened after that was sedate in comparison. Anderson, the $600,000 bonus baby who was starting his first game as a pro, ran for two more touchdowns. Two field goals inflated the lead.

After the game Vince Lombardi returned to his home.

On Olympus.

LEW ANDERSON: He talked constantly about playing a game that was free from error, physical and mental. The one game that came closest to that was the 55-7 victory over the Browns. The Browns were a good team but on that day the Packers were close to perfect. Vince was delighted.

December 9, 1967

The Rams had to win. It was just that simple. Losing meant wait until next year.

The Packers did not have to win, which is not—in the case of a Vince Lombardi team—to say they did not have anything to lose.

They had a lot to lose if you listened to Vince Lombardi. Like pride, for one thing.

He brought his team to Los Angeles five days early and he took it to Santa Barbara to work. Eleven months earlier he had brought his team to Santa Barbara to work, too. That time it was for the Super Bowl.

The Packers' record was 9-2-1 and they were champions in the Central Division. They were assured of being the host team in the Western Conference title game.

The Rams were 9-1-2, a record that would have led any other division in the NFL except the Coastal, where the Baltimore Colts were 10-0-2.

For Los Angeles, the mission was mountainous: The Rams had to beat the Packers and then they had to beat the Colts the following week.

Part One of Mission Seemingly Impossible began in routine fashion. The Packers scored a touchdown in the first quarter and the Rams scored a touchdown in the second quarter. At halftime, the margin was a field goal. Green Bay led 10-7.

The Rams took command in the third quarter. Roman Gabriel and Jack Snow collaborated on a touchdown pass for the second time and a field goal from Bruce Gossett made it 17-10. The pendulum appeared to have swung the Rams' way.

Looks can be deceiving, however. Because scoring against the Packers in 1967 meant you had to kick off to the Packers and kicking off to the Packers usually meant that you had to kick to Travis Williams.

Williams had returned three kickoffs for touchdowns earlier in the season and this was to be his fourth. A run of 104 yards enabled the Packers to pull even.

The Rams got a field goal early in the fourth quarter to go ahead again but Chuck Mercein, the discarded running back, put the Packers in front with a four-yard touchdown run. It was 24-20 and only 2:19 remained.

The Rams could not move then and they punted. The resistance was matched when the Packers had the ball and on fourth down Donny Anderson was back to punt. Tony Guillory rushed through to block it and Claude Crabb recovered for the Rams on the 5.

There were 34 seconds left to play when Gabriel passed to Bernie Casey for a five-yard touchdown and the improbable victory.

The Packers had lost but they had fought the good fight. Besides, there was one thing they hadn't lost. Their self respect.

BOYD DOWLER: He detected signs of slackening off in practice that week. The game meant nothing to us because we had our division clinched. But he had us running sprints and doing pushups up in Santa Barbara. He told us, "You don't have any pride. You're a disgrace to the National Football League."

DICK BOURGUIGNON: Of course we read in the papers that the Packers were resting up for the playoffs.

WILLIE DAVIS: As far as our season went, the game meant nothing. We had our title. But the Rams didn't have theirs and he didn't want them to have it, either. Before the game he said, "I wish I could go out there today and play this one myself. Then I'd be sure I'd get it done the way I want it." He took the losing that day hard.

JERRY BURNS: He got mad in the coaches' room afterwards. He said, "Goddammit, I wanted this one!"

JIM MURRAY: When Vince Lombardi loses a football game, particularly with the numbing suddenness he did that day, it is wise to enter his locker room with a whip and a chair. Not that day. Vince Lombardi's face was suffused with pride. All he had lost was a game. But he hadn't tried to sell the Green Bay Packers with one wheel missing or the engine failing. He hadn't come into town with a plastic team craftily disguised as the real thing. His team lived up to the warranty and no one wanted his money back. No one hollered for the Better Business Bureau.

"My father is 80 years old and not in the best of health so I call him often to see how he is. I called him Saturday night and I said, 'Pop, how you doing?' and he said, 'Well, you sure blew one today, didn't you?'"

December 23, 1967

They said he never wanted to win a game as badly as this one, this rematch with the Los Angeles Rams, this game for the Western Conference championship.

They said he said this was the game they had to win. And maybe he did. Vince Lombardi said the Green Bay Packers had to win a lot of games. This merely was one of them.

But what a *one* it was!

On the surface, the Rams appeared to be the best team in pro football. Their record was 11-1-2 and in winning their last six games of the season they had averaged 30 points a game while limiting their opponents to 10.

The Packers had lost their last two games—the first to the Rams on a blocked punt, the second to the Pittsburgh Steelers.

And so they said that maybe the Packers were getting old. Some people even said that the Rams were the team of tomorrow and the Packers were the team of yesterday.

For a time—for barely over one quarter—it did seem like that. The Rams got a touchdown when Roman Gabriel passed 29 yards to Bernie Casey (the same combination that had felled the Packers two weeks earlier) and two Packer drives were ended by lost fumbles.

The futility was given additional extension when Chuck Lamson intercepted a pass by Bart Starr, and early in the second quarter the Rams seemed ready to take 10-0 command on a 24-yard field goal by Bruce Gossett.

The play that turned the game around was made by linebacker Dave Robinson. He batted Gossett's attempt into the ground. With it went the hopes of the Rams.

From that moment, the game belonged to the Packers and in the last 3½ quarters the execution was a microcosm of everything Vince Lombardi ever had talked about.

Bart Starr completed 17 passes in 23 attempts for 222 yards and one touchdown. Travis Williams rushed 19 times for 88 yards and two touchdowns. Henry Jordan alone sacked Gabriel four times.

Old men, huh? The team of yesterday, huh?

Phooey.

JERRY ATKINSON: This game was being played in Milwaukee and there was a lot of wonderment about that because if we hadn't won that game Green Bay would not have had a playoff game at all the following week. I thought, wow, that's really confidence.

¶ It was on a Saturday afternoon and he came in a couple days before that, into my office, and he said that he had been searching for something to motivate these boys. He finally came up with it and I can't quite quote it exactly. It's from the Scriptures and it goes – something like this – "Many run the race in the arena but one man wins." And he had this thing stuck up there in the locker room.

JACK TEELE: When we came out to work out on Friday afternoon I looked around the place and there was Lombardi sitting there alone up in the empty stands. We didn't want him watching us so I headed up there. Just then our team came running out on the field, bare-headed, wearing only their warm-ups. And so I climbed those stairs and when I got close to him – he was staring at me – he said, "I'll say one thing. The Rams certainly lead the league in sideburns." He turned around and stalked off.

WILLIE DAVIS: By the time we took the field the Rams were like a group of people coming into our homes to whip us in front of our families. He painted it so clear that by the time each of us took the field we were ready to defend everything. I mean, like there was Charlie Cowan in front of me and I'm saying to myself that there's nobody going to whip me in front of my friends, my family. Lombardi had told us that if these guys could whip you here they could whip you anywhere – even on Sunset Boulevard. He said the Rams are here to challenge your existence as a man. He said the Rams would like to feel like they can destroy or intimidate you and for that reason you gotta dislike all they stand for. So it wasn't just like another game. It was like you were playing out of an arena for a lot of things, some bigger things than just winning or losing.

He had us so high for that game it almost scares me. I remember before the game how Bob Skoronski – I think it was him – stood up and said, "Coach, just don't say any more. No more." And then Skoronski turned to me and said, "I'm going to kill that Lundy."

75
15
10

DICK BOURGUIGNON: So the Rams beat us out there. And the Rams beat the Colts the following week. So we had to face the Rams again. And you know the reputation they had with that front four. This man wanted that game – he never wanted one more – and he had this ball club so ready for it. That, I think, was one of the most perfect ball games ever played. He thought that, too. He had to sell our team that they could do it and he had to leave no doubts. And so we got out there and we ran right at those guys, at Jones and Olsen, right from the start. "That was the closest thing to perfect," he said later, and, gosh, it was!

BOB SKORONSKI: Every time Marv Fleming lined up he would be tight with Forrest Gregg on that side and they would double team Deacon Jones whether we passed or not. Basically, we just took Fleming out of our passing game. And this so confused Jones that day that after the first quarter we didn't even need to do it anymore because every time Fleming lined up in there, Jones was fearful of the double team and he'd go out and around and he couldn't have gotten back to the passer if he'd wanted to.

BOYD DOWLER: He was very proud of our game plan for that game. It was his idea to take away the Rams' pass rush by double-teaming Deacon Jones and Lamar Lundy on pass plays. He had Marv Fleming playing really tight. It confused the Rams –

"I was proud of them after the game in Los Angeles but I've never been prouder than I am today."

all this moving around in the offensive line – and they never were able to adjust.

BART STARR: He had a great deal of compassion. He sure did. I've seen the man so choked with emotion after a ball game he couldn't even speak. He would get so welled up with tears he couldn't say a thing. We would say the Lord's Prayer after the game and if you were anywhere near him you could see that he was fighting to get it out. When we beat the Rams in that playoff game in Milwaukee he walked in after the game and he could not talk. He said something like, "I'm so proud of you I don't know what to do." I tell you, he just barely got that out.

December 31, 1967

tick...tick...tick.

The Dallas Cowboys lead the Green Bay Packers by three points with 4:50 left to play. The Packers have the ball on their own 32. They are 68 yards from a touchdown that would win a third consecutive National Football League championship. It could just as well be 268 yards. The Packers have had the ball four other times in this half and they have done nothing. There is no reason to think they will do something now. It is 13 degrees below zero. There is 4:50 left to play.

tick...tick...tick.

It is that way on this day, a day on which they play football on tundra, on which 50,000 people sit in a football stadium in Green Bay and try to keep from freezing to death.

There is hope, faint hope. There is Donny Anderson taking a pass in the flat. There is Chuck Mercein going seven yards on a sweep around right end. Oh, that Packer sweep! But then Chuck Mercein is not Jim Taylor, is he?

There is Starr hitting Boyd Dowler over the middle for 13 more yards and then Anderson coming back after losing nine yards to take a pass from Starr to gain 12. There is Anderson and Starr teaming again, this time for nine yards to the Dallas 30. Two minutes are left.

tick...tick...tick.

There is Starr back to pass again. His hands must be freezing just like everyone else, right? They *must* be freezing. Starr passes and it is Mercein again. In this same year Chuck Mercein was rejected by both the New York Giants and the Washington Redskins but now it is Chuck Mercein eluding tackles and crashing 19 yards to the 11.

And there is Mercein again, this time taking a handoff from Starr and glancing off left tackle to the 3. Maybe Chuck Mercein *is* Jim Taylor.

tick...tick...tick.

There is Anderson smashing down to the 1 and then into the line again and again and getting nowhere. There are 20 seconds remaining and Starr calls a timeout. He goes over to talk to Lombardi. They have no more timeouts left and it is third down. They could try a pass and if that fails they could kick a field goal that would tie it. Then they could take their chances in sudden death. Or they *could* gamble.

Play resumes. There is Starr over center...

tick...tick...tick.

Starr keeps the ball and he moves behind the wedge of Jerry Kramer. He is into the end zone and it is all over. The Packers have it. They have won by a score of 21-17. They are champions again, for a third time in a row, for a fifth time in seven years. There are 13 seconds left on the clock.

tick...tick...tick.

JIM KENSIL: I told him that Dallas was coming in on Friday and that they wanted to work out on the field on Saturday. He said, "They can't work out Saturday. We've got the field all lined and we won't have time to re-line it." I said, "It's a championship game. They *have* to work out. If we can't find anybody to re-line the field, Don Weiss and I will get some guys off the street and we'll do it ourselves." So it became a real shouting match. Finally I told him, "Okay, uncover only half the field. To the 50," and he said, "I won't uncover it past the 20." I thought that, well, this is silly and I figured that I'd just come back in the morning and tell him how it would be and just as I was getting ready to say goodbye he said, "Hey, how about meeting me for dinner?" Just like that. A whole new tone of voice. And so I went out with him and a couple of his close friends and we're having a great time. There's been no talk of any kind of football. All of a sudden he turns to me and says, "We can turn it back to the 50 Saturday." It was that simple.

TOM LANDRY: I noticed the change in him. The pressure that third year – for that third in a row – was tremendous on him.

TEX SCHRAMM: He had a lot of little kid in him. When we went up there the day before to practice he had this electric grid laid underneath the field and even though they had completed their practice he waited around until I came because he wanted to show me. He was just like a little kid with an electric train. He had the panel of switches there and he showed me how you turn it on and how you warm this part of the field and that part of the field and how the thermostat controls it all. He was just so excited about that thing and this was the day before playing for a world championship. I said then to him, "I don't know if you would be more disappointed if your electric grid doesn't work or if you lost."

JIM KENSIL: I ran into Willie Davis in the lobby of the Northland that morning. He had leased an apartment in Green Bay so he had been staying in the hotel that week. I said, "Man, it's gonna be cold out there," and he said, "Yeah," and he blew on his hands. He had gloves on and he said, "I sure wish the man would let me wear these today," and I said, "Aw, he'll let you wear 'em today." Willie said, "No way. He'll say, 'You can't grab 'em as good with gloves on.' I can. But that's what he'll say."

JIM KENSIL: It was 16 below in the morning and we were concerned with whether we could play or not. Our concerns were two: We didn't know about the damage cold weather might cause to the players and we really weren't sure what the fans could take. We talked to the Dallas doctor and he said he wasn't worried. He said the only danger was in frostbite and that could be minimized if socks were changed often and other common sense was followed. We wanted to talk to the Packers' doctor, too, so Mark Duncan and I went into the Green Bay locker room. We told Vinnie we were going to ask Dr. Nellen about it and he said, "What do you want to talk to a doctor about it for? The weather's beautiful. The sun is shining!" He talked about it as if it were nothing and then he rushed us over to show us the panel for the electric device that was heating the field, all the dials and meters. "I don't know what you guys are concerned about," he said. "It's a great day!"

¶ I was with him until an hour before the game began and then I said, "I'd best get upstairs." He said, "Where are you going?," and I said, "The pressbox," and he said, "Dressed like *that?*" I had a regular topcoat on. I wasn't worried. I was going to be in the pressbox and, anyway, I'm not really bothered that much by cold weather. So he said, "You're a damn fool kid"—this was just a couple hours after he'd told me what a nice day it was—and he said, "You haven't got any more sense than to go out in the cold dressed like *that?*" Then he bellowed, "Phil!," and when Bengtson came running he said, "Get this guy some sweat socks." Then he wanted Bengtson to get me some sweat pants and a sweat shirt and I said, "Naw, I'm not gonna run around like that." He said, "Get out of here then. I can't do anything about stupidity."

CHUCK LANE: I had to go in there and tell him that the heating system had failed and that his field had frozen. I never heard such a bellow in my life, almost as though I had destroyed his heating system. I just told him that I was out there with the grounds crew and I had come back and it was just like kicking an airport runway it was so hard. The tarp actually had deceived him. The heat had come up and hit the tarp and water had formed on the tarp and then dropped down on the field, so it was moist. When they pulled the tarp off it was beautifully soft and his system had worked tremendously

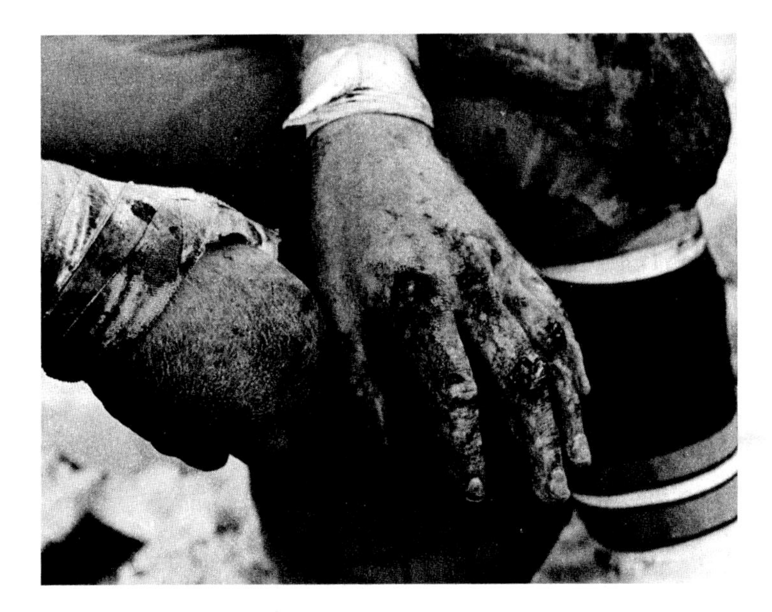

but it flash froze and it was just as hard as a rock. My gosh, his toy had failed and he was so sure it was gonna work. He said if it didn't work it would always be known as Lombardi's folly. When I told him that day he bellowed like somebody had stepped on his corns and he rushed out there to look.

VINCE LOMBARDI, JR.: The field just froze up like an ice cube. I was with him when he found out and he was just sick. "They're gonna say that I did it on purpose," he said. "They'll never believe what happened."

HENRY JORDAN: I figured Lombardi got on his knees to pray for cold weather and stayed down too long.

JIM KENSIL: I was standing in the pressbox when the Packers ran on the field and I looked through my glasses. They weren't wearing gloves.

TOM LANDRY: The thing that develops character in people most times is adverse situations. In other words, the discipline and conditioning programs they went through, the punishment and suffering, they all tend to develop character. And once you get character then you develop hope in all situations. That is the great thing that comes out of it. And Vince developed a lot of character in his players, character that a lot of them probably would never have had without the leadership and discipline he developed in them. Therefore, they never were out of a game. They never felt like there wasn't some hope. And that is what carried them through to that third championship. That is what beat us.

CARROLL DALE: If in the fourth quarter you are behind, you are going to run harder. In other words, if you are behind, everyone has the motivation to win. So losing never entered my mind that day. We had a chance to do it, and we did. So in a case like that you just think about the things you've got to do. It's fear and worry – and there were a lot of people in Green Bay who ran because of fear. You just pushed yourself. And someone came up with the big play. That's the way it was in the cold. That's the way you do it when everybody really is motivated.

BOB SKORONSKI: When it began, when we were 67 yards away or whatever it was, we were gathered together on the sidelines and someone said, "Well, we got it." That's all anyone said. We didn't do a lot of shooting off at the mouth.

¶ We never made another plan beyond that point, beyond Bart's touchdown. We just assumed it would work. If that play had not worked the clock probably would have run out because we had nothing else called and I don't believe we'd have gotten another play off.

"This is what the Packers are all about, the way we came back."

ZEKE BRATKOWSKI: You talk about simplicity and execution, to me one of the greatest game plans as far as execution was the Dallas game. The passing game and running game went just like the plan we had drawn on the blackboard. I commented to Bart and to Coach Lombardi after the game and Bart and I were saying, boy, coach, it was a great game. It was just super. It was just like all week we went over and over and over it. And it paid off. In the last strike, when we went for the touchdown, it was one of the great drives in the history of football. With the middle linebacker isolated on Donny Anderson, Starr hit Donny in there twice and then Bart caught Chuck Mercein in the flat. Chuck caught the ball and he ran down in there, to scoring territory. That Mercein catch was a very good example of the Green Bay passing game. Lombardi's theory was to stay away from that middle linebacker if he was strong.

TOM LANDRY: He never discussed it with me but I think that deep down he always believed they would win.

"We went for a touchdown instead of a field goal because I didn't want all those freezing people up in the stands to have to sit through a sudden death."

TEX MAULE: And then someone told me, "Hey, Lombardi was talking in the next room and he started to cry," and I didn't believe it. Vince Lombardi cry? And so I went in there and when he saw me he turned around and wiped off his face. When he turned back his eyes were red.

CHUCK LANE: He wouldn't admit that his players had frostbite. Ray Nitschke's ears, toes and fingers were white and the skin was falling off those guys by the yard. But it wasn't frostbite. His people didn't have frostbite. Only the Cowboys got frostbite.

"The Dallas Cowboys got frostbite. Ray Nitschke just had a blister. Only a blister. That's all it was. A blister."

RAY NITSCHKE: I damn near froze my toes off. It was a miserable feeling.

VINCE LOMBARDI, JR.: I rode home with him after the game. He was really pumped up, more so than usual, and he told me that I had just seen him coach his next to last football game. I think I was one of the first people he told.

ART DALEY: The happiest I ever saw Vince was at the New Year's Eve party the night of the 13-below day. God, he was on the verge of tears all night.

JOHN KOEPPLER: I said to him that night, "When you think about it, you had to take the field goal and a tie." And he said, "Those decisions don't come from the mind. They come from the guts."

TEX MAULE: We had some terrific arguments about it later. I said that in that situation you have to try a pass and then if that fails then you kick a field goal and at least get a tie and a chance at sudden death. And he said, "That is bull, mister. If you can't run the ball in there in a moment of crisis like that, then mister, you don't deserve to win."

"We were very pleased with the way the heating unit performed. Next year it will be perfect."

83
Starr
15

January 14, 1968

Super Bowl II was like some eerie carbon copy of Super Bowl I.

Close quarters for 30 minutes. No contest after that.

The Packers won by 25 points over Kansas City a year ago in Los Angeles. They won by 19 points, 33-14, over the Oakland Raiders on this day in Miami.

It was, too, more a victory for method than for emotion. The emotion was there for the Packers on the Sundays of two and three weeks before in Wisconsin, when the opponents were the Rams and the Cowboys. It was not on this Sunday.

But then it didn't have to be.

The Packers were threatened only momentarily. After assuming a 13-0 lead midway in the second quarter, the Packers allowed the Raiders to move within six points when Daryle Lamonica passed 23 yards to Bill Miller for a touchdown.

Don Chandler's third field goal made it 16-7 at intermission but the spark clearly was missing. It was in the locker room then when Jerry Kramer told the team. "Let's play these last 30 minutes for the old man." They had heard rumors about his retirement. Everyone had.

And so they rose up in the last two quarters and not for a moment was there any doubt about the outcome. When Herb Adderley dashed 60 yards to a touchdown after intercepting a Lamonica pass it was 33-7.

It was to be the last derring-do of the Packers under Lombardi. He had ended the way he had come in nine years before.

Exactly 141 victories later.

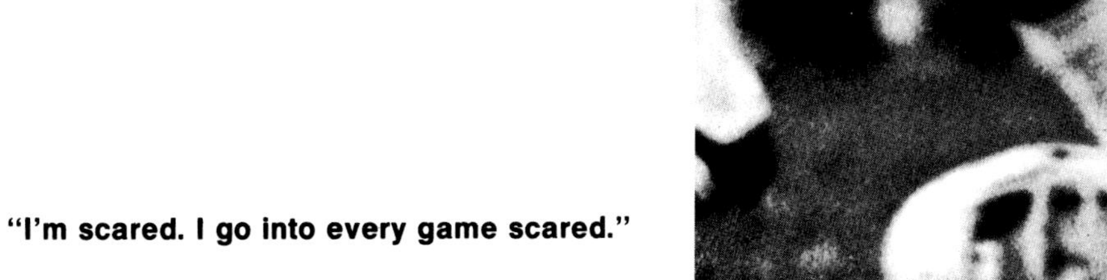

"I'm scared. I go into every game scared."

MARIE LOMBARDI: He had a terrible head cold the week before the game, coming off that game in the 20 below weather – or whatever it was. The doctor gave him some medicine to clear up his head and a couple days before the game we were going to some function with Col. Krueger and his wife and Vinnie said, "I don't know what the doctor gave me but I feel better already," and the taxi driver turned around and said, "Good God, man, don't you get sick!" We all laughed about that because obviously the guy had a lot of money bet on the Packers. And you know that 2½ years later, when Vinnie was in Georgetown for surgery, we got a letter from that same taxicab driver reminding him of that incident in Miami and saying he'd pull through the same way now. It was very touching.

CHUCK JOHNSON: Lombardi was short with newsmen the year before, in California, but he was astoundingly mellow that week in Miami. He handled one difficult situation beautifully. A Miami sportscaster grilled him relentlessly one day at a large press conference and no one quite knew what to do. The sportscaster was blind. Lombardi was gracious, brilliantly gracious, and he finally offered to see the man privately at the end of the press conference. When the conference ended Lombardi was given a warm ovation. That was a first!

JACK TEELE: He cooperated like crazy, went through all kinds of interrogations. He knew a lot of the writers anyway but those he didn't he would say, "Who is the guy, third down on the left side of the table?" And his players reacted to the press with total cooperation, too. Very big league. You felt that he told them, hey, that's part of our job, too. We are in show business.

ZEKE BRATKOWSKI: When we played Oakland in the Super Bowl we knew they played a lot of bump and run and we had never been exposed to that other than the Bears. So we went to Miami and the first day we got out there early. We brought out some defensive backs, we got some ends and Bart and I just stood there and threw sideline passes all day. And we would go back and throw even before the guy would turn. And we kept doing it, doing it, doing it. We didn't throw a lot in that game but the ones Bart did throw were complete. That was Lombardi precision.

BART STARR: He was dressed in a business suit one day, which was totally uncharacteristic of him because

he never let anything get in the way of football. He was going to a reception and it followed closely on the heels of our afternoon meeting. So he got up to say something to us, about what a tough year it had been for us and how he had admired the courage that numerous players had displayed and that it had been a trying year because we had suffered adversity and injuries and so forth. He said, "It just goes to prove what character you really have," and the longer he talked the worse it got and he got so choked up that he just had to sit down and turn the projector on.

HERB ADDERLEY: After the game I walked up to him and said, "Congratulations, coach," and he gave me a big smile and a big hug and he said, "Congratulations to you, too." He was crying.

ED BRESLIN: So we go over to the Kenilworth and I've got this suite all set up and I've got six bottles of champagne there. There's no one else but us there and he says, "How about we open one of those?" He never drank champagne so I'm wondering what's up. I pour two glasses and he says, "Here's to my swan song," and me, I almost drop my glass. He says, "This is it, Eddie. This is the end."

Players

“That word ‘selflessness’ as opposed to ‘selfishness’ is what I try to teach.”

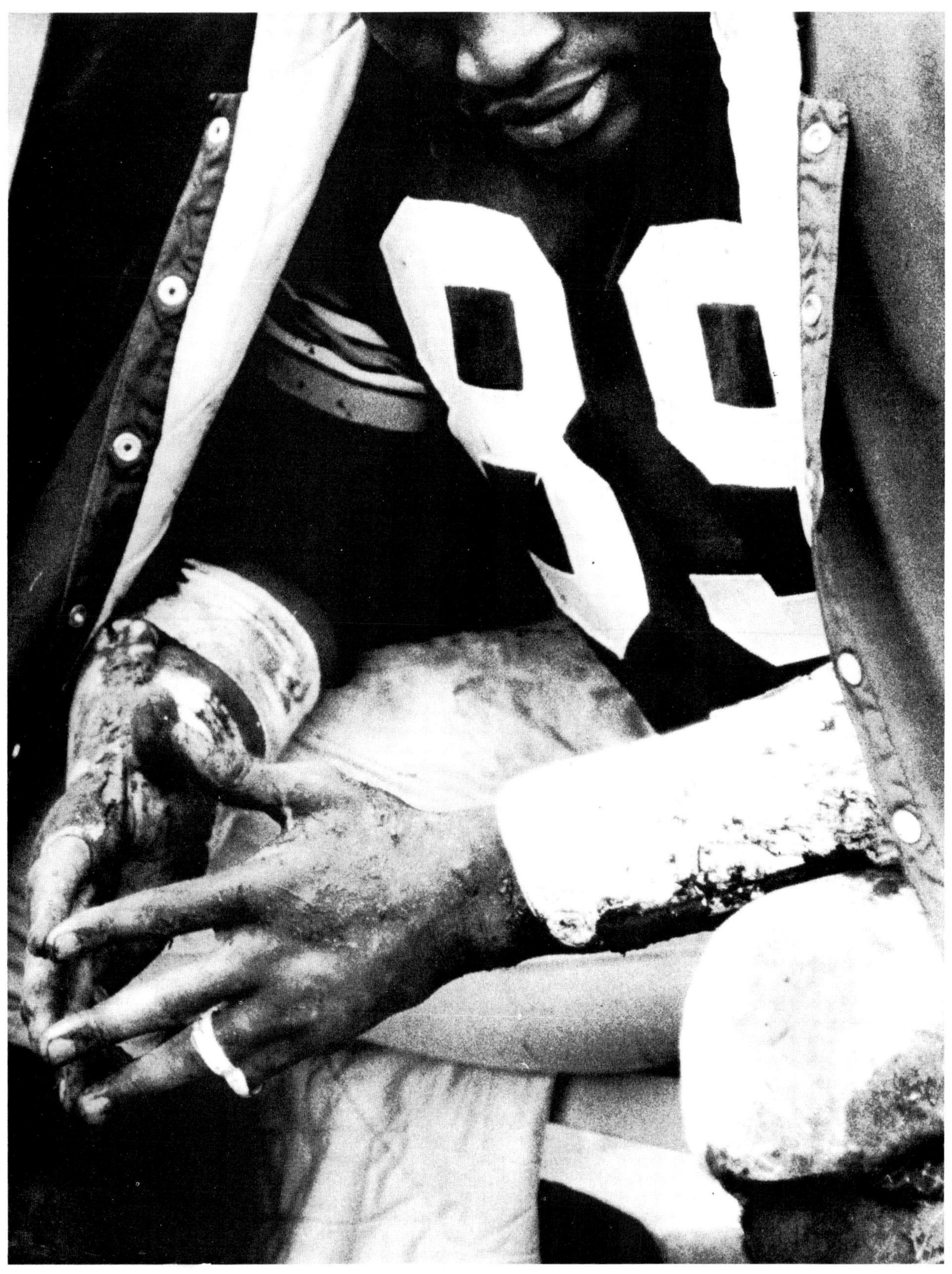

Dave Robinson

"Some guys play with their heads. That's okay. You've got to be smart to be No. 1 in any business. But more important, you've got to play with your heart—with every fiber of your body. If you're lucky enough to find a guy with a lot of head *and* a lot of heart, he's never going to come off the field second."

Players: his first love

MARIE LOMBARDI: I came in second best in the love department. His first love was his precious Packers.

DICK BOURGUIGNON: There were times when he'd use the word "family" when he talked about his football team.

MAX MC GEE: He could get the best out of more people than anyone I've known. It wasn't just Starr or Hornung. He could get the best out of the 40th man on the squad. He could get the best out of a secretary. Or the bus driver. You'd get on the bus to the stadium and that driver was alert. He was ready. Everyone was performing better than he had previously and you could feel it all through the Packer organization.

JIM RINGO: I think another thing that Vince had that not many coaches have is that he was able to take a man who nobody else knew where to play and play him. He took a Henry Jordan, a Willie Davis, a Ray Nitschke, a Herb Adderley, a Bob Jeter – there are many more than you could name: Fuzzy Thurston, even a Ron Kramer – when everyone else was starting to give up on him. Oh, and Paul Hornung, Jimmy Taylor, Bart Starr. He sure had this extra sense where to place people and how to use them.

FORREST GREGG: What did we contribute to the Packers? Well, our bodies for one thing.

Paul Hornung

Paul Hornung

EMLEN TUNNELL: Paul came back from an Army Reserve meeting once to play in a Thanksgiving Day game in Detroit. He had to stay up all the night before just studying plays because he hadn't been to practice for awhile. Paul didn't carry the ball more than a couple times that day but he blocked for Taylor – blocked like hell. He was so tired and black and blue when it was over that they had to cut the uniform off him. Vinnie really appreciated a thing like that. A player'd do that and Vinnie would never forget him.

PAUL HORNUNG: You know I always wondered myself why he liked me so much. I think that vicariously he would have liked to have been in my position – you know, the good life, a bachelor and all. Maybe. I don't know. I do know that the year or two after I was gone Jerry Kramer and I were talking and Jerry said, "God, how the old man misses you!"

EARL BLAIK: I was there one day after a game with the Bears. I don't remember who won but I do remember that Paul Hornung had not had a particularly good day. Vinnie said to him, "That Heisman trophy – that's no big deal, is it?"

DAVE SLATTERY: He loved to tell the story about Paul Hornung getting on the bus in Green Bay and just making it. The bus was leaving and he jumped on and he had lipstick on the side of his cheek and Lombardi, who was always in the front seat on the right in the bus, said, "Where have you been?" All the players were shaking. And Hornung said he had been to church and he kept right on going to the back. And Lombardi said, "Church! How do you like that? He's been to church!" It just broke him up.

DICK BOURGUIGNON: I think his biggest disappointment with a player was when Paul Hornung let him down. When the commissioner called Lombardi, Vince said, "Don't do anything until I've had a chance to talk to Paul. I'll find out." So he talked to Paul and Paul said he wasn't involved. Vince went to bat for him then. And Paul had lied to him. That was his great disappointment. But to show you the character of Lombardi, he also felt that when this guy came back if he was to be traded or just left sitting it would ruin a good person. He stayed with this man and as a result there wasn't anything that Hornung wouldn't have done for him. The suspension actually brought them closer together as it turned out.

PAUL HORNUNG: The suspension in '63 hurt him more than it did me – and it killed me. It was like we'd let each other down.

¶ In 1964, the year after I came back from the suspension, I really stunk up the place. I peaked too early and I couldn't do anything right after the first four games. I just was unable to lock my ankle properly for kicking and then it started to psych me, I know. The only thing he ever said to me about it was one day when he said, "Stick with it." When you were down, he didn't drive you down deeper.

¶ I consulted the man on just about everything and I remember going to him one year and telling him how these people – I don't know if they were Democrats or Republicans – had come to me and wanted me to run for some office, county clerk or something like that. There really wasn't much work involved. You just had to show up once in a while to sign some checks. I said, "It looks like stealing to me," and he said, "You'd be a damn fool if you took this. In the first place, if you're going to get into politics, get in at the top, not the bottom."

¶ I didn't play in the first Super Bowl and since I'd been banged up pretty bad – my shoulder, especially – we figured there was no way an expansion club was going to waste its money. We figured wrong. Vince put me on the available list and the Saints picked me up – figuring on me, I guess, as a hypo for season ticket sales. He called me from Shor's and I could tell that he was mad and broken up. He said, "That was a dirty trick they pulled. If I'd had any idea they were gonna take you I wouldn't have put you on it. I'm really kicking myself."

Hornung/McGee

CHUCK LANE: He had a liking for characters like Hornung and McGee. They were his kind of people. I think Vince often would have loved to have said, "Oh, the hell with it," and gone out and had a few beers with those guys because that's the kind of guy he was. But he couldn't allow himself that pleasure.

ZEKE BRATKOWSKI: Guys like Hornung and McGee could say things at meetings that some people would never have gotten away with. But because of the way they presented things and how funny they were and being great football players, they got away with it. Like there would be a lot of times when they'd be downfield on a pass and they'd give him kind of a pig Latin or double talk thing and he couldn't hear them and he would

Jerry Kramer Paul Hornung

Fuzzy Thurston

say, "What in hell did you say?," and they would come back with what they had really meant to ask him. The players knew they were putting him on a little bit.

PAUL HORNUNG: We found out later what set him off. It was Saturday, August 3 – in whatever the hell year it was – and about 10:30 that night Marie calls Vince at training camp and when he gets to the phone she says, "Happy anniversary!," and slams the telephone in his ear. So now he's been shown up and squelched and he's looking for some fall guys. He'd chew up the first guy in his path. So at 11 o'clock McGee and I walk into our room and at 11:01 Lombardi busts in and says, "For this little scene, 250 bucks each!" We couldn't believe it. It's true that you're supposed to be in bed with the lights out at 11 o'clock during training camp but it's also true that this was a Saturday night and also on Saturday nights the married guys got to go home to their wives. I mean to tell you we did some yelling back and forth but his final comment is "Horseshit!" and he stomps out of the room. I was really fed up and I says to McGee, "Let's get the hell out of here," and he says, "Yeah," and we pack and we're going to leave for Miami. Max had a helluva an idea, too. He said we could sell the story to *Look* or *Life* for at least $10,000 each. It was a natural. All the while we're getting steamed and packing. Jerry Kramer and Jim Taylor were there, edging us on and then saying we didn't have the guts to go. Then McGee starts getting rational and he says, "Well, maybe we ought to stay overnight – you know, sleep on it," and me, I go to the bathroom, and when I come back my bag is gone. By then I'd decided not to go by myself, anyway.

¶ Max and I went to see him in Washington just before the season began. We were sitting around their house in Potomac – we'd had a nice evening – but we had something else scheduled. We had an appointment to meet some people! So we thanked them and said we had to leave. Vince liked that. He laughed and said, "You guys haven't changed at all. You're still sneaking out on me at 11 o'clock."

Max McGee

Howard Ferguson and I dropped into training camp during rookie week – we were both veterans – and we made the mistake of having lunch with the team. That night we went back downtown to the hotel we were staying at because we weren't due to check into camp for another week. We had our first meeting with Lombardi that next day. Actually, it was a screaming

Max McGee

match. He yelled, "If you want to eat with this team you'll work out with them, too!" Right then I knew it was going to be a long summer. But I guess I must have been pretty impressed with the man because I checked into the dorm that day.

¶ I was the type that if I wanted to go out and get a couple drinks and chase a broadie around the block, well, I just went. He always caught me, though. Every time. And he fined me heavy. Other guys might get $100 for missing curfew but he knew I didn't give a damn about $100 if it was time to bust out so he'd hit me with something like $500. He might get on me for breaking curfew on say a Tuesday and then the rest of the week we'd ignore each other. Then about Friday he might come over to me as we were going out to practice and just nudge me a little or tell me some absolutely horrible joke. It was a gesture to say that the fight was over and I'd always accept the truce.

¶ He knew some guys had to be pushed and he rode them unmercifully. Like Jim Taylor was the backbone of our team but he had a tendency to let up unless he was ridden all the time. On the other hand, Lombardi knew that I didn't play so well if I was being screamed and hollered at. I don't like to be embarrassed in front of other people. He found out all about me quickly. He found out about all of us.

JACK TEELE: When he took over the Packers, in the first camp, he caught Max McGee out after curfew and he told him that the fine would be 250 bucks. And he told Max, "The next time I catch you it'll be 500 bucks and the time after that it'll be $1,000." He said, "Max, if you can find me a woman who's worth $1,000, let me know and I'll go with you."

PAUL HORNUNG: Vince took a lot of kidding about his clothes. When he'd get a new suit – which wasn't often – he'd get on a bus and strut around, really proud. Once he gets on with this really dull gray thing – maybe sharkskin or something like that – and he sticks out his chest and says, "How do you like this, huh? 325 bucks!" And McGee says from the back of the bus, "I sure hope you got some change when you left the store."

MAX MC GEE: I could make him laugh and I know he liked me because of it. He'd back himself into an emotional corner and I'd let him get out of it. Like that stretch in '65 when we were winning but doing zero offensively. After we won 6-3 on two field goals he was furious. He told us to forget everything he'd told us, to scrap it all, that we were going back to the basics and fundamentals. He reached down and picked

Paul Hornung Jim Taylor Bart Starr

Bart Starr

up a football and he said, with the great sarcastic grin all over his face, "This is a football." And I said, "Slow it down a little, coach. You're going too fast."

Bart Starr

JIM KENSIL: I met him for the first time in March or April of 1961 at a meeting and we went out for dinner that night. The title game with the Eagles was still vivid in my mind and I asked him how he felt when Bart Starr didn't see the receiver wide open and waving his arms. I think it was Max McGee. Vinnie said, "Yeah, some guys see them and some guys don't." Then he said, "I'd like to get that guy Meredith." He told me that he had offered the Cowboys, who had just played their first season, any two players on the Packer roster. I said, "*Any* two?" He said, "Any two." He really didn't think that Bart Starr was what he wanted in a quarterback. It was interesting to me later when Starr started seeing *every* receiver. I always meant to ask Vinnie what happened to that two-for-one deal.
BART STARR: He came back here in June, before his first operation, to make an appearance at something or other. And he stopped by the house and we were sitting in the den and chatting. It was the most relaxed conversational experience we'd ever had with the man, I guess because he never really had that kind of time to spare. And it was in our home under very pleasant circumstances, totally removed from football, and we were talking. And he said to Cherry and I how happy he was for us and he remarked about our home and how he thought it was so beautiful. And Cherry said, "Coach, as you know, we owe most of this to you." I swear you could see his eyes well up.

Jim Taylor

SAM HUFF: He had this entire reel of plays we called 36 Slants and all the plays were from the Green Bay days, most of them great shots of Jimmy Taylor. There was this one run that was from the Super Bowl game with Kansas City and you can imagine that Lombardi must have seen that film a thousand times. Well, he ran it back four or five times – he was standing in the back of the room operating the machine – and there was Taylor on the screen bouncing off a guy and heading for the outside and knocking down another tackler and Lombardi said, real loud, "Look at that son of a bitch run!"

JIM TAYLOR: Every player in pro football is capable of having the basic techniques to play football. They know how to tackle. They know how to approach a block. They know all the fundamentals of a perfect

Jim Taylor

Bart Starr Ray Nitschke Willie Davis

block. They come out of college and they know that. It's the motivation that's the thing and he knew just the right words, just the right approach to me. He knew how to handle me just like a parent handles his children to get the maximum out of them. Just the right approach to get me to listen, that was it. And he motivated me to the maximum. I don't think I could have given more.

¶ We had a real feud going on for awhile, after I signed with the Saints in '67. But then we met each other again when the Saints played the Packers in Milwaukee in '68 and there was a real outpouring of emotions. I sat with him and Fuzzy and Hornung up in Vince's private box. We talked about old times.

DOM GENTILE: The year after Taylor had played out his option, in '67, the coach comes to the training room. He came in and he sat down and he had a real weary look to him. He just looked real depressed. He said, "By God, if Jim Taylor was here my problems would be over." And then someone else, I forget who, said something like, "If it weren't that problem it'd be another problem," and Lombardi said, "Well, you can say what you want about that boy but he can still play football."

Willie Davis

I think we had a closer relationship than he had with most players because a lot of the things I had to live with, the desires, the things that were important, they were things he had lived with in his life. There were many times when I'd go into his office and he'd close the door and we'd have a really deep philosophical discussion. He talked about the parallels of his situation and mine. He felt that because he was Italian he'd been held back for a long time and he said that's the way it was for Negroes now. He said, "If you really want something" – and he felt I did – "you can have it if you are willing to pay the price. And the price means that you have to work better and harder than the next guy." He was not bitter when he talked about his past. I think he used it with me to show that he had great empathy for the problems of blacks all over.

ED BRESLIN: There wasn't an ounce of prejudice in Vince. He loved Willie Davis and once we were talking about a racial thing and someone mentioned that Willie was a model black man. Vince got mad and he said, "You know I really don't know what color Willie Davis is. And I don't care."

Ray Nitschke

EMLEN TUNNELL: Oh, that Nitschke was crazy as hell. He had the locker right next to mine. Tom Bettis was the middle linebacker then so Nitschke didn't play much. And Ray used to get on Vinnie about it. He'd say, real loud in the locker room, "Just call me the judge. Just call me the judge. 'Cause I'm always on the bench." Ooh, that would make Vinnie mad. He gave Nitschke a lot of hell. He was trying to help the guy and he did. He changed his whole life around after I left the team. But Vinnie knew the guy was going to be a football player. He *knew*. He handled Ray Nitschke just right.

MIKE MANUCHE: Vinnie really did a job on him! He would say to him, "We don't need you!" But he saw something in him and he really straightened him out. Ray had trouble expressing himself sometimes early in his career and he would become violent and tear everything apart. Vinnie taught him how to express himself in other ways. He turned that energy to football.

PAUL HORNUNG: Once in a nutcracker drill Jimmy was the ball carrier and Nitschke was supposed to stop him. There was very little running room because the dummies were up there tight and the blocker – some rookie – just screened Nitschke while Taylor slid by. Vince stopped the drill and said, "Mr. Nitschke, I have read that you are the best linebacker in the NFL but after watching you just then I find it hard to believe. Now, do it again!" This time Ray grabbed the rookie by the shoulder pads, literally lifted him up and threw him into Jimmy. All Vince said was, "Next group." It took them two minutes to get the rookie to come to.

CHUCK LANE: In the course of an evening – when Ray was slightly over-served – he would start pitching folks through the windows of saloons and breaking bar stools over peoples' heads. He did a lot of things that tended to discourage business.

¶ Times sure change. Ray Nitschke is a model citizen today. The reformed barroom destroyer is now encouraging children's savings accounts with a Green Bay bank.

RAY NITSCHKE: He helped to turn me around as a person. He inspired me by his determination in what he did. He set an example I chose to follow.

Emlen Tunnell

They were doing a story on me and there were cameras everywhere – in the locker room, on the practice

Ray Nitschke

field. We were getting ready to play Pittsburgh and I was going out on a pass to cover Gary Knafelc. The ball was thrown way out of bounds so I didn't chase him. Vinnie came storming up to me and he said, "You don't wanna play. You don't wanna play! Get off this field! Go in!" I was mad as hell and the players were mad at him, too, because the ball was way out of bounds. So I walked off. After practice he didn't say a word. All those cameras around the place. They were getting on my nerves and maybe they were getting on his, too. But the next day at practice, the next morning, he came in and he said, "Emlen, you mad at me?," and I said, "Hell, no, but you act like a high school coach." He said, "Are we still friends?," and I said, "Yeah," and we shook hands. We laughed and that was it. It took a helluva guy to do that. When he came up to me the full squad was there and he talked real loud. I know that just impressed everyone, him being head coach and all.

¶ He told me I wasn't going to play in a preseason game so I snuck out one night. Hell, he knew I'd snuck out. Don't ask me how he knew but he always did. This was the night before the game. That next day against Dallas he stuck me in there right at the start and he never did give me a break. I looked bad but he taught me a helluva lesson. Which is something because I was 36 years old at the time.

¶ In the three years I was in Green Bay he picked up my hotel bill at the Northland. He didn't have to do that.

¶ I got married after I retired in '62 and I came around the College All-Star game in Chicago that year. And Vinnie said, "You kidding? You really get married, Emlen?," and I guaranteed him that I had. He said, "Son of a gun!"

Boyd Dowler

One Christmas, in the first couple years there, he asked Hornung and his mother and my wife and I over to his house for dinner. He came up to me on the sidelines before practice and he asked me what my plans were for Christmas Day. I told him that my wife had bought a small turkey and we just were going to have a small dinner. He said, "Well, think about coming over to dinner." I said I'd check with my wife that night and let him know. So practice ended that day and I'm walking off the field and he sidled up alongside me and he said, "Listen, I think you'd better come over Christmas. I'll tell Marie." Just like that. I felt we had to be there. It was an order.

Emlen Tunnell

Boyd Dowler

¶ In 1963 after I'd had two bad games, he said, real loud, "I can go down to the high school and find guys who wouldn't drop balls." But then he eased off. That year I had a bad streak of dropping them. I was lousy in games and in practice. But he stayed with me. Finally he called me aside and he said, "I know what you need. You need a big game to get your confidence back. Don't worry about it. It'll come." The next Sunday I caught eight passes against the Vikings and I finished the season strong. I gained over 900 yards that year and most of them came in the second half of the season. I'll always believe it was because he didn't give up on me.

Jim Ringo

DICK BOURGUIGNON: When Jim Ringo was traded to Philadelphia he was the most surprised and disappointed man in the world. He came in with this agent and this guy started making demands for Jim. And Vince told this fellow he didn't want to talk to him. He said he wanted to talk to Jim. So they bantered back and forth and Ringo ended up saying, "Either I get this kind of money or I want to be traded." So Vince said, "Okay, we'll see what we can do about it." They were planning on a Jim Ringo Day and a lot of things that year and he went and traded him. He traded away an All-Pro center. He said, "To hell with it. Let's show them who's boss here." I don't think anybody tried to call his bluff on the ball club after that.

JIM RINGO: There has never been a man — and it will be a long time before I *do* meet a man — that I will love or respect as much as I did Vince Lombardi. I would have liked to have had this man for my father. There was no way I could fail him — because he would not allow me to fail. He was that type of man. You wonder if he had any shortcomings. He was a religious man and a dedicated man and a family man. And he believed in his country. Where else can you find a man with all these convictions and yet lived by his conscience? He is the most important person that I ever met. He's done so much for me that nobody else could ever do. I'll tell you the way I feel about it: I hope my son meets a man along the path of his life like Vince Lombardi. He would do so much more for my son than I could do for him. With a son, you have a lot of emotions. With Lombardi, it wasn't emotions, just hard, cold facts.

Fuzzy Thurston

EMLEN TUNNELL: When Fuzzy came to us in the pre-fall

that first year he was always hurt. He always had some bandages on. Always something. We were getting ready to have our intrasquad game before the last cut and Vinnie says to Fuzzy one day, "Dammit, Fuzzy, if you don't play today you're going home. You're always hurt. You're always complaining." That really frosted Fuzzy, made him furious. He tore off the bandages and he said, "I'll show that son of a bitch." Fuzzy didn't start the scrimmage that day but he got into it early and he played well. He never looked back after that, either. Who knows? If Vinnie hadn't given him hell I'm just about sure that Fuzzy Thurston would've been cut that next day.

CHUCK LANE: Fuzzy was always the guy who'd grab the mike or who'd get up in the aisle of the plane and entertain everybody. Vince loved that.

PAUL HORNUNG: We kidded Fuzzy Thurston about being short for a lineman and one day Fuzzy turned to Vince, who was even shorter, and said, "You don't have to be tall to be great, right coach?"

FUZZY THURSTON: When I became involved in the restaurant business, Vince wasn't too happy. He felt that your life should be football all the time, that you should think of nothing else – just like him.

¶ He asked me at a banquet after the '67 season, after the second Super Bowl. He said, "Fuzzy, when are you going to announce your retirement?" That hurt me because I thought I still could play. But I quit anyway – because I'd never known him to be wrong. Ever.

Zeke Bratkowski

He would get on me for some reasons I couldn't figure out why – because I was playing ball extremely well. Maybe I would make a few mistakes – misthrow a pass or misread a key or something – and he would really let me have it. I can remember him coming to me after practice and he would say, "I just want you to keep the bit in your mouth. I just want to keep you ready. Your practice was great but I just want to keep the bit in your mouth." So I told him, "Coach, it's bleeding already!"

¶ When I first came here, Fuzzy and Jerry and those guys, when I'd call a running play they'd say, "No good, Zeke," and I began to pick up their thinking on it – pick up *his* thinking on it! They knew that the automatic had to come because that play was no good against a stacked defense. They were so trained they anticipated it. And so I really became schooled into recognizing what was happening before the play even started.

Forrest Gregg

JIM RINGO: Forrest is probably the finest offensive tackle I've ever seen. He's got finesse. He never blows up under pressure. He never gets excited – he does everything with his head. He's got all the prerequisites. So you just know that he was Vince's kind of football player.

Elijah Pitts

I played two games for him with a shoulder separation. In college I wouldn't have dreamed of putting my uniform on. Here, I didn't dare tell him I had it.

HERB ADDERLEY: Elijah Pitts, Ernie Green and I came to the Packers in the same year and the three of us were rookies and all of us were offensive backs and at the time they had Tom Moore, Paul Hornung, Taylor and a few others. Lombardi knew that the three of us couldn't all make it. I had a no-cut contract, being a No. 1 draft choice. I knew I was going to be there one way or another. Pitts came out of the South and he didn't know anything about life at all. Ernie Green did, going to Louisville and all and here's Pitts from a small college and without the coaching that Ernie had had. So what Lombardi did was trade Green to Cleveland. He knew Ernie would get a chance to play a lot of football there and he kept Pitts so he could help him with life and football. We knew and Lombardi knew that Green was a better football player. But this was a case where Lombardi saw potential and he wanted to be involved in its realization.

DOM GENTILE: During one training camp after an extremely bad day of practice, in the evening meal the rookies were asked to do their singing. This particular batch of rookies were very poor singers. Lombardi began to bristle until finally Elijah Pitts, a veteran, got up and sang a fantastically beautiful song. Lombardi stood up after he had finished and said, "Eli, you just made the ball club." Because of the wealth of offensive backs at the time, there had been serious question whether Pitts *would* make the team.

Herb Adderley

He always said that a defense was built around cornerbacks. And he always preferred a man-to-man defense. Looking back, I think the main reason for that was that if you played a zone it was hard to isolate one man and blame him for a pass reception. In a man-to-man it was easy to pick out someone to yell at. He did some yelling at me, too, but he'd

Forrest Gregg

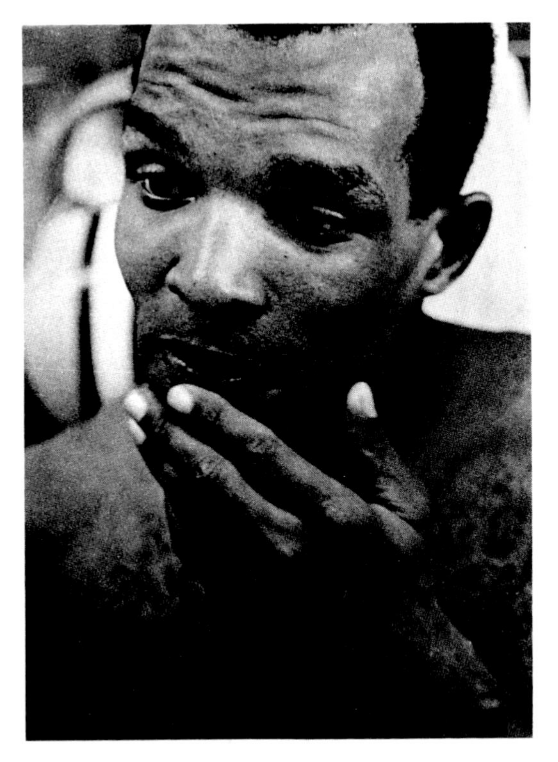

Herb Adderley

say some nice things, too. Once he told me after we played a good game against the Bears, he said, "You played the best game I've ever seen a cornerback play." That was the best compliment I ever got. Oh, and he also said – this game was on national television – "I'm sure the people who saw that game, I'm sure they feel the same way. Keep this in your mind, that each time you go on the field you say to yourself, 'I want these people when they leave here to say to themselves that they saw the best cornerback they have ever seen.'" So each time I go out on the field that's what I think about.

Tom Brown

I think that he always appreciated the fact that I played baseball. He always liked baseball, Lombardi did. He liked to watch it.

¶ I played when I was hurt. It was just a dislocated shoulder. He didn't forget that.

¶ I depended on him to motivate me, to get me to play. When he wasn't there Bill Austin or anyone else just couldn't do that.

Lee Roy Caffey

PAT PEPPLER: Lee Roy is big enough and strong enough and tough enough – with speed, too – but he's lazy. He needs to be pushed. The first day he stepped on the field in Green Bay – I was standing right next to Phil Bengtson – and Lombardi told Phil, "You get on that big lazy turkey right now. He's walking around here like he's got the ball club made. He's lazy and we're gonna have to push him." This was the first day! And about that time Caffey walked by and Lombardi said, "Never mind, I'll tell him myself." And he said to Caffey, "You listen to me. You don't have this ball club made by a long shot. You might not be here five minutes, you big turkey." Everybody on the field heard it and they started calling Caffey "turkey". He took this fellow and he turned his whole attitude around. He made some big plays for those championship teams.

Lee Roy Caffey

Lionel Aldridge

I thought he could better have served his purpose by being a teacher, working in some place where he came in contact with a lot more young minds. And he would have had the opportunity of molding and shaping and helping some of these people to form some definite opinions and definite ideas and goals for themselves. This was the biggest impression he had on me. When I came here, I was kind of a flaky kid, really. I had a hard time getting along with people because I was moody and didn't really know what I wanted. And I didn't really have too many plans for myself. He made it a complete turn-around. Not by taking me aside and telling me a bunch of words. The guy did it, more or less, by example. He lived exactly how he taught.

¶ He would belittle you in front of your peers but you didn't have to feel too bad about that because you knew that all your peers knew that their day was coming. Because of that – who knows why? – I never felt close to him. Maybe because he wouldn't let me. But when he was gone, there all of a sudden seemed to be a tremendous void someplace. Something that I wouldn't have any more. Something that I had really enjoyed and something that I had drawn a lot from. And that was suddenly gone. And I found myself going back over all the years I had played for him mentally. And I was around him and tried to remember particular incidents that were impressive. No matter where I was at, no matter where my memory went, I was tremendously impressed.

Carroll Dale

My happiest memory is the day I was traded there. And being able to meet him. To have him say, "Welcome." To just have the privilege of playing for the guy.

¶ To Lombardi, discipline just meant putting forth a greater effort to win and you welcome discipline when you see the results. I've played for many coaches in my time and I'd have to say, quite honestly, that as coaches many of them were as good as Lombardi. But the thing Lombardi had that set him apart was the ability to make each guy on the team feel confident. He made me believe in myself. He made me understand discipline and self-discipline. He showed me the way to win.

Willie Wood

Ron Kramer

PAUL HORNUNG: The list of men he helped is long and I'm near the top of it, of course. But one real special case was Ron Kramer. Vince didn't motivate Ron immediately but that's part of the beauty of it all. He came to us, Ron did, with an I-don't-give-a-damn attitude. He had great ability and great confidence in it but he just didn't use it. For a long time, he wasn't able to do the job. Vince got on his ass something terrible. He never let up and then one day, after nearly two years of that I guess, things just went click,

click, click and Ron Kramer became a magnificent football player. He told me that in high school and college no one ever raised a voice to him, that it had all come so easy. Well, things sure changed. When Ronnie made it to the top he thrived on the shouting. Once – and this was a couple years after – Vince really let loose with some fire on a Wednesday or Thursday and Kramer sat by his locker shaking his head. I asked him what the matter was and he said, "I don't know how the son of a gun does it, but I'm ready to play right now."

Willie Wood

I think the nicest gesture he ever gave to me was not really saying too much to me.

Larry Brown

You know I'm not really sure he knew who I was until one day in a nutcracker drill – that's where you have to prove that you're his kind of man – he had two big sandbags squeezing two big linemen together. When Sonny handed me the ball I blasted between them before they could raise up. Right there in front of God, Sonny, the two linemen and the two sandbags, the coach stopped practice and said, "Nice going." It was the most extravagant praise that had come out of him since he took over the Redskins. From that day on I thought I had a chance to make his 40-man squad if I worked at it.

¶ I had some troubles catching the ball that first year. I was nervous and I told him so and he said he couldn't have that. He said, "Backs have to catch the balls like ends or we'll get somebody who can." He concentrated on one remedy – relaxing my hands. "Make a big thing out of doing only one thing," he said. "Watch the ball. Overexaggerate watching the ball and leave your hands limp as it comes in. Relax and you'll get it." It worked like a miracle.

¶ He was the one who first noticed that I might have a hearing problem. He got on me but I told him that between learning his system and reading defenses, even Einstein would forget the counts sometimes and have to look at the ball. The coach smiled at that and then he told me to get a hearing test. He noticed that I was like 1/50 of a second late coming off my stance. He was right, like always. It was my hearing, something no other coach had ever noticed. He had my helmet outfitted with the hearing aid and I haven't had a problem since.

Sam Huff

I was working for the J. P. Stevens Co., selling fabrics, and I saw this film, "Second Effort." I'm an emotional person and I heard that music and that voice and I was sold. I knew I had to work for him, work and play for him. I took a cut in salary to do it but I never for a moment regretted it. The year with him was a treasure. It was like working on a doctor's degree.

¶ Once we were talking about motivation and he said, "You know I'm not really sure I'm reaching these players here. What do you think?" And I said, "I don't know, coach, you're reaching me," and he laughed and said, "You're easy to reach. Anybody can reach you!"

Sonny Jurgensen

I walked into his office in Washington not knowing what to expect. After we shook hands he looked at me and said, "Sonny, I want you to be yourself. Just be what you are." What a thing to say! Jeez, right then I felt like running into a wall, anything to let him know I would do whatever he wanted of me.

I learned to love him. I learned more in my first five days of listening to him than I did in 12 years of listening to other coaches.

Larry Brown

Sam Huff

Sonny Jurgensen

Home

**"Only three things should matter to you:
Your religion, your family and the Green Bay Packers.
In that order."**

Green Bay
Packers

Harry Lombardi

MARIE LOMBARDI: The happiest day of my life was the day I met him. Jerry Kramer said to me once, "You didn't start to live until the day you met him and I didn't either."

CHUCK LANE: His father was a hard-driving, crusty man. His father would call him if the Packers were defeated and he would just give Vince a terrible dressing down on the phone about how shabby his team looked and about how they lacked discipline and they lacked this and they lacked that. Like it was *his* fault.

DR. ANTHONY PISONE: He and his father shared a stubborn streak. Once Vince told his dad not to fix the roof on the house, to call a professional. Vince arrived home that afternoon to literally find his dad hanging by the eaves. Vince gave the old man hell after he got him down.

TEX SCHRAMM: Marie was the greatest needler of Lombardi of anybody I knew. She chopped him down. When he was being the big hero and starting to order people around or telling her off or anything like that, why she would always have some kind of remark that would just break you up and he'd break up, too, because she'd have him so dead to rights.

Home: where the closets were

CHUCK JOHNSON: Once when we were practicing for a 49er game in Palo Alto, Marie went to Lake Tahoe for the day with some friends. When he found out that night he was furious. "How'd you get there?," he yelled. Now she was mad, too. "We flew," she said and he said, "Over the mountains?," and she said, "No, *under* them, you dummy!" Honestly, they both went from rage to laughter in an instant.

DR. ANTHONY PISONE: Once in Washington he was surrounded by six beautiful girls. Marie had to laugh. She said, "Look at America's newest sex symbol!"

MARIE LOMBARDI: I always knew how far I could go with him. And of course he knew the same with me. I learned a lot about him and his pride in our 30 years. I used to make him say he was sorry but I learned later on that he was more important than my silly little pride. The last 15 years or so he never had to say he was sorry for anything around me.

TOM LANDRY: I think it would have been difficult for him to have had any really close friends, ones he'd confide in. I think that Marie was the one he confided in. To operate the way he operated it takes control. You just can't open yourself up because you are always on guard, always demanding certain things. When you do that you can't relax very often.

Marie Lombardi John Lombardi

OCKIE KRUEGER: Vince always talked about his big yard and his nice home and all that but I would say conservatively that he didn't know a blade of grass from a sunflower. He never turned over a shovel of dirt in the yard. I don't think he could run the dishwasher, the washing machine or anything else. The one thing he could do was cook. He was an excellent cook but when it came time to clean up the dishes he would always laugh and say, "That's not my department."

MARIE LOMBARDI: I could tell what day it was just by his mood. Monday, Tuesday and Wednesday we didn't talk. Thursday we said hello. Friday he was civil and Saturday he was downright pleasant. Sunday he was relaxed most of the time.

JERRY ATKINSON: After the games we lost, Marie was the one trying to change the pace that had been set by the gloom. She could do it real well. I'll never forget the time we were upset by the College All-Stars. Vince was fit to be tied. She went around to all the tables and talked to the people and was very gracious. She allowed people to smile.

OCKIE KRUEGER: Ten days before he was due to go to the Redskins' camp for the first time the phone rang about 5:30 one afternoon and Marie said to me, "What are you doing?," and I said, "Nothing." And she said, "Well get over here quick and let's go out for dinner. He's started cleaning closets again."

MARIE LOMBARDI: Whenever there was an important game or some kind of crisis, he would clean out closets. Or attack the basement. He would take everything out of the closet and pile it in the middle of the room and then he'd look at me and say, "What in hell do I do now?" So I'd usually end up putting everything back.

In June, just a few days before he was hospitalized for the first time, LeRoy, our chauffeur, arrived at the house and began emptying all the bookcases downstairs. This was a couple hours before a party I was giving for the Redskin wives. LeRoy insisted that Mr. Lombardi had told him to go home and empty those cases. So I called Ockie. "My God," I said, "now he's even got *LeRoy* emptying things out!"

VINCE LOMBARDI, JR.: He could never sit through an entire movie. We'd go to a movie – always a western – when I was a kid but he could never stay to the end. "Enough of this," he'd say and then we'd have to go.

¶ My whole childhood was spent constantly being

on guard. I couldn't get into any kind of trouble because what would people say —"He can control his players but he can't control his kid."

¶ He never really encouraged me to play football. Never directly, anyway. I guess it just was always understood. You can imagine that my father being who he was that people expected a lot of me. Like when we moved to Green Bay in 1959, before my senior year in high school. I was about the same size then as I am now — about 5-10 and 170 or so. When I got to Green Bay I suddenly became 6-2 and 215 and they offered me a choice of high schools and some of them even offered me cars. I just wanted to play football, maybe not for the right reasons, but I guess because it seemed the thing to do. I know my father took an interest. When I was a freshman at St. Thomas College my father told the coach to open the gates on me to see if I could take it. He meant for only a limited amount of time. The coach thought he meant for the whole season. So every day I'd be sent off to a corner of the field with one guy who weighed about 210 and another who went 190 and we'd go two on one all afternoon. I'd be the one and they'd be the two. I was in tears when practice ended every day. It took all the fun out of it for me.

¶ He never saw me play that much but in those games that he did I always seemed to have my best days. But even if he wasn't around, he seemed to have his eye out. When I came to St. Paul for my sophomore year, I really had forgotten to get a room the year before. I wasn't trying to pull a fast one to get off campus. So I got in with an apartment with some other guys, a neat place. My father found out about it and he called the dean of men and he said, "This is Vince Lombardi. Send my son home." So I was forced to move back on campus — or else. I was just furious. Well, it developed that about five of the guys who lived off campus went down the tube that year. And I wound up on the dean's list. It was that kind of thing that made me think that maybe he knew me better than I knew myself.

¶ Oh, the jobs he would line up for me during summer vacations then. I bet I was the only guy in college who didn't look forward to summer vacations. My father would find the dirtiest, rottenest job he could for me in the summer. Loading box cars with pickles and relish, construction jobs — oh, man, the worst!

¶ You know the way he felt about injuries. He didn't feel any differently about them when it came to me. I mean like I really had a bad knee and it gave me a lot of trouble when I was a freshman in high school, back in New Jersey. It was a case where I couldn't trot but I could go full out so I'd limp when I was trotting but not when I'd go full out. So it looked like I was dawdling. And I hurt it again and I had to get carried off the field when he was there. The next day we were going to New York. I played on a Saturday and we drove in the rain to the Polo Grounds the next day. He gave me a long lecture about faking injuries and it really hurt me. He said that he did it once or twice but that he never was proud of it. That really hurt me.

There was another time, too, when I got hurt pretty badly. I got cut up on the face. It was nothing really serious but it bled like a gusher. My mother climbed down out of the stands and crawled under them to where they'd taken me to make sure I was all right. My father was there that day, too, and boy did he give her hell for doing that. He told her I wasn't a baby anymore.

One time I hurt my knee pretty bad at St. Thomas in my freshman year. I stretched a couple of ligaments. I didn't tear anything but there were about four or five days in practice when I honestly felt terrible. So I really babied it. I took treatment but I just lay around. That went on for about two weeks back at school and then the Packers came up to Minneapolis to play Dallas in an exhibition game the second or third week in September. This was the year before the Vikings had a club. I knew the Packers really well, of course, so I went to the hotel and limped around and got a lot of sympathy. I was feeling pretty good then and I went up to my father's room and he had some people in there for cocktails. This was the Saturday before the game. It was in a suite and he called me into his bedroom. He said, "Come in here!," and I came in and he had the doctor look at me and the doctor told me there wasn't anything wrong with my knee, just some stretched ligaments. Then I had to listen to my father and, wow!, you wouldn't have believed it. He told me that I was going to have to run on it tomorrow, that there was nothing wrong with it, that I was babying myself. I cried. But I ran on it the next day.

¶ I guess I was about 22 years old, maybe 21, and I was in law school. Well, I came home for a weekend and rushed out without saying hello and met some friends of mine I hadn't seen for awhile. We went out drinking. I was feeling pretty good but I knew I couldn't do it all night so I came home about 9 o'clock and I sat down and watched television. I was sitting there and my father was sitting there and he said, "You smell like a brewery. Get to bed!" I was 22 years old and I got sent to bed by my father. I went.

MARIE LOMBARDI: I ran on Lombardi time, too. He never was late in his life. Hostesses hated that but he said, "Dammit, if the invitation says 6 o'clock then I assume they mean 6." So we always got to parties on time but then we got into a routine of driving around the area until someone else showed up. We got tired of always being the first ones there. Once it was snowing and we were driving around when we had a flat tire. We ended up walking three or four blocks in the snow, yelling at each other all the way. He spent the whole night entertaining people with that story. Another time there was a party for Edward Bennett Williams, a birthday party, I think. We were there on time and it was getting dark so we sat in the car and waited for other people to arrive. They did and – my God! – the men were in tuxedos. He said, "Why didn't you tell me it was black tie?," and I said that I must not have read the invitation properly. So we started back to our place – clear across the city. We were shouting all the way and I told him it didn't matter what he had on, that there'd be a lot of people there in business suits. So we went back and when we got there some more people were going in and all the men had tuxes. We turned around again and there was more shouting. All the windows were rolled up in our car but I can remember a car pulling alongside us at a light and a guy looking over at me and saying, "You're right!" Well, you won't believe it but we ended up going back to the Williams house again and it was the same thing all over. Then we went home. We never did get to the party.

OCKIE KRUEGER: There was a routine every December 24. I'd call up Prange's, the big department store in Green Bay, and tell them he was coming – and to watch out! They knew about how he was and, golly, the store used to fill up with people just watching him shop. He'd walk up and down the aisles with the store manager and as he'd pass a counter he'd say, "I want one of those! And one of those! And one of those!" He'd buy 75 presents in an hour and every time, when he was done, he'd expect that each thing he'd picked out would be gift wrapped.

MARIE LOMBARDI: He loved to give. Christmas was a very big time for him. One year he gave me 10 little boxes and one big one. I had to open the small ones in a special order and he had clues leading up to the big one: a mink coat!

He was the same way on other big days, too. Like our wedding anniversary – if he didn't forget. He was very secretive about it but sometimes he wasn't very subtle. Shortly before he went in the hospital the first time, in June, he said to me, "Not that I'm going to buy you a ring, but what's your size?" Our 30th wedding anniversary was August 3. Things happened so fast then that he never got around to getting anything. But I found a jewelry store card in one of his shirt pockets later and I knew what it was for.

FRANK COWLES: Vince was a lousy mechanic. He had trouble changing a burned out light bulb. One Christmas I stopped by his house and helped him put toys together that he had gotten for his grandchildren. I'm sure that if he had taken the time to learn he could have. But he didn't have the time. He'd sit there and laugh amid all the gadgets and screws and wires and say, "What kind of crazy person dreams up stuff like this?"

VINCE LOMBARDI, JR.: He came over to our house when they were here to play the Vikings. We used to drag them over, my mother and him. He really enjoyed the kids, he really did. He had that voice – oh, that voice! – and he used to walk behind them and yell "Hey!" He really scared the pants off them. My eldest wouldn't go near him for a long time. My father really felt bad about it. For a year or so you could see him try to smooth relations. And of course he did.

TEX SCHRAMM: I was riding with him in his golf cart when they had the twins, his daughter. Marie came out in another cart and told him. She was half crying and he was the same way. He got up on the tee and just whammed it. He was so proud.

JIM KENSIL: We were talking about kids one time. Basically, my feelings are that you should be strict with kids. I remember saying to Vinnie, "I really don't care if they like me but I do care if they respect me." And then I said, "Besides, I think if they respect you then they like you, too." He smiled. He said, "You're absolutely right. And the one thing you can't have in dealing with kids is common sense. If you use common sense you have to let them do anything."

MIKE MANUCHE: He was like a 1918 father or something. The children had to do this and this. He said, "They may not love you at the time, but they will later."

John Lombardi   Vince Lombardi, III

¶ Vinnie and his son were just getting close to each other. In the last year, his son was beginning to realize what a helluva guy his old man was.

VINCE LOMBARDI, JR.: He never did get his law degree — he only needed a few more credits — so it really was a big thing to him when I got mine. I mean when he was proud, really proud, he didn't have to say a word. His face told it all. He used to introduce me as, "My son, the lawyer." And one of the last times I saw him, in the hospital, I had a conservative suit on and he said, "You look like a lawyer."

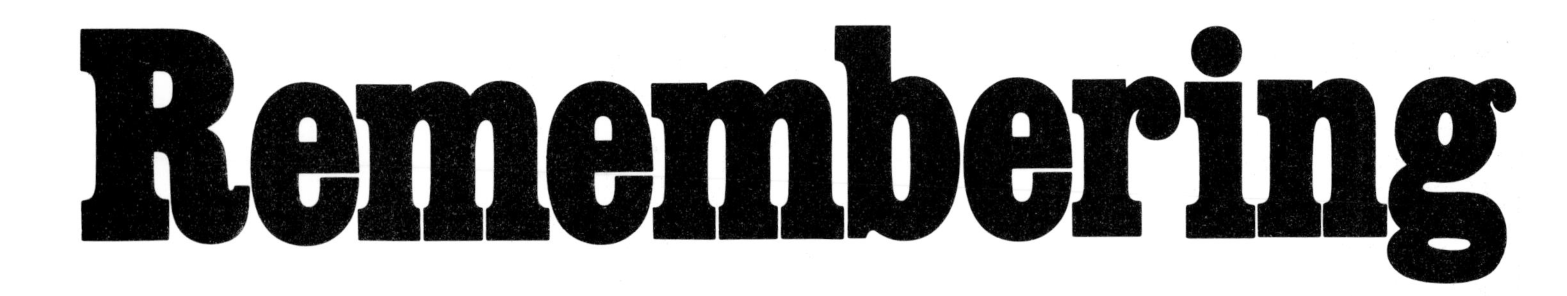
Remembering

"If we would create something we must be something."

"As a person, I am not well enough adjusted to accept a defeat. The trouble with me is that my ego just cannot accept a loss."

Remembering: the memories

LIONEL ALDRIDGE: He wasn't all things to all people but he was something to everyone.

MARIE LOMBARDI: Basically, the story of his life is a dull one. He was a very simple man, very shy, never good in a crowd. And he hated publicity.

WILLIE WOOD: He was the general and we were the privates. You didn't ever go over his head because you couldn't. There was nobody to go to.

EARL BLAIK: He was a commander in the truest sense of the word.

JIM RINGO: The man who didn't think he got a fair shake from Vince Lombardi had better look at himself first.

MARK DUNCAN: The guy who never suffered the wrath of Lombardi was somebody he didn't want to waste his time with.

¶ No matter how mad he got he never stopped thinking. That's something. His mind always was going. And it seemed like the more angry he got the harder his mind worked. Maybe anger made him focus his mind better.

SAM HUFF: I'd been around football for a long time but he got more out of me than I ever thought I could give.

DR. ANTHONY PISONE: He had a really bad arthritic knee. He suffered a lot during the last few years. But he

didn't complain. That would have been out of character.

CARROLL DALE: The thing that I remember most about him is that he was very much interested in the total man as far as his players were concerned. I know that he was very interested in the fact that guys be total citizens. In other words, that we not only be good football players and winners, but that we be the type of people, you know, citizens the town would be proud of. He also taught us unselfishness and brotherly love. Those are the very words he used. Oh, he could be tough verbally at times. His tongue could be very cutting but yet he was a guy who could be serious one minute and laughing and having fun the next.

JERRY BURNS: It was religion in the morning and the language of a longshoreman in the afternoon.

FATHER DAVID RONDOU: What guided him most was fair play. He coached and he did everything with that in mind – a recognition of the other man. In other words, you could almost use the word justice. If it was right, if it was just, well, then he'd go ahead with it. If it was wrong or unjust he wouldn't do it. And then, too, he was a prudent man. He used common sense in all things.

EDWARD BENNETT WILLIAMS: To call Vince Lombardi a fine coach is like saying that the Louvre is a well-constructed building in Paris.

SONNY JURGENSEN: He could have made a success out of the Edsel.

TEX MAULE: He used to read himself to sleep with Thomas Aquinas or original Latin. Among coaches, that alone put him out of the ordinary.

JIMMY CANNON: He kind of encouraged his image as a rock – tough and pious.

¶ I think that he became the leading man in his own fantasy. It was genuine. Lombardi took himself very seriously. If he had one fault, I would say it was that, but yet this was part of the reason for his success. Like the Jesuits, he believed in great inner strength. I don't think it's any coincidence that he once studied for the priesthood.

CHUCK LANE: It was like in the Old Testament, the rule of fear. It was like he was omnipotent and omnipresent. Yeah, fear. But it was effective.

JIM LAWLOR: I took my two friends in with me to meet Vince and we were sitting there having a few drinks, having a helluva time, and he looked down at me with that big smile on his face and he said to my friends, "You see that big Irish bastard down there? We've been friends for well over 30 years and you know what he's done for me in 30 years? Nothing." And he said, "You know what I've done for him in 30 years? Nothing, either. That's the way we both like it. We don't do favors for each other and we like each other." I think that was the nicest thing he ever said to me.

NORB HECKER: He always called me Norb and I always called him Coach. I just could never get up enough nerve to call him Vince to his face.

OCKIE KRUEGER: I always used to say about my bosses in the Pentagon, the good ones could sleep at night. And *he* could sleep at night, too.

BOB COCHRAN: He could have run General Motors. Maybe not the overall thing but he could have taken a division and whipped it into shape if it were lagging in sales or production. Like in his own offices. He computerized the operation. He built new offices and he made the whole organization look as if it were the slickest thing going.

BILL CURRY: When I left the Packers, I said that he coached by fear. Later, I thought about it and now I can look back and realize that the reason I resented him was that he was making me grow up when I didn't want to. He was thinking of me.

EMLEN TUNNELL: I betcha a lot of the guys he coached didn't really like him. But they all respected him.

LOU SPADIA: If he'd been a truck driver, he'd have given 110% there, too.

JIMMY CANNON: He was an original – like Hemingway's writing style or the singing of Sinatra or the Beatles.

JIM LAWLOR: How many people know that every time he spoke and got that thousand dollar fee that he gave it all to charity? He charged $1,000 to discourage people and when they wanted to pay it he gave it to charity.

HOWARD COSELL: Lombardi had an excellent mind. He had an excellent scholasticism that he did not really employ. He employed his scholasticism limitedly later in his life, after the successes. When he was asked to appear before organizations like the American Management Association, he sat down and, face to face with himself, tried to relate that which he was, which he was doing, to something broader. On the gridiron itself, in the daily flow of coaching, the daily urge for winning and, indeed, the *need* for winning, there inevitably came a point when there was a decline in the use of scholasticism. He reached a point, as I guess any man does, really, where he was so absorbed by the daily exercise of his function – and especially if you believe in it, as he did – that he didn't find the time to be scholastic, to be abstract, to be philosophically detached. The football successes grew and utterly absorbed him to the point where his whole life was a series of duly constituted maxims that he successfully imparted. So men would actually believe that they had more to give than they ever really had to give in the football sense. Of course, that was his great quality of leadership.

¶ In the society in which we live, the nature of his contributions, his growing importance, certainly transcended. In the minds and hearts of many people in this country, he became more than a football coach. Industry sought him out, so did government, so did educators. They felt he had much to contribute on campus.

BART STARR: He stood for principles and qualities that are considered corny in our society today. I think the majority of people are neither far left nor far right. They are just shadows on either side of dead center. I think that these kind of people would identify with a man like this. You will find leaders on the far left who have followers and leaders on the far right who have followers, but not the huge masses. To me, Coach Lombardi would gather the masses behind him and people would want to identify with someone like that.

BUD LEVITAS: When the big flag craze started, he came to one of Marie's birthday parties with a whole handful of flags. He pinned one in my lapel and he said, "You stand up and be proud of your country. You wear this forever."

EDWARD BENNETT WILLIAMS: When Spiro Agnew laced the press, he just loved it because he had a lot of suppressed hostility for the press himself.

DUDS BILOTTI: If he had gone into politics he would have been a helluva president. In fact, if he had to deal with Khruschev taking off his shoe and pounding it on the desk he probably would have pounded him on the head with his own shoe. I can see him talking to Khruschev and people like that but after they got through he'd probably trade them. Or put them on waivers.

OCKIE KRUEGER: We were out at his house one night and one very prominent person started talking about how these kids needed to express themselves when they tore down the flag from the Department of Justice. The man said, "If you tried to stop them it would be stifling their freedom of expression." Vince and me, we just got all over him. Vince said, "Those kids should be spanked," or something like that.

TEX SCHRAMM: I remember what somebody said when the hippies or whoever they were stormed the Department of Justice and broke windows, when everyone went up to Washington. They said they would have liked to have had Lombardi as the attorney general and have him come out that door and see what the hell would have happened then.

VINCE LOMBARDI, JR.: The kids that are coming up now and complaining, he just didn't know what to do with them. He got very upset the last year in Washington when a couple of boys he signed for automatic bonuses just up and quit. I'm not so sure that he could have handled it the way kids are coming up now. Like Namath. My father liked Namath. He thought he was quite a guy. But he couldn't accept what he stood for and being associated with football and all. My father ranted a lot about Namath and talked about getting the police after him. With my father, either you did it his way or else. I think kids today don't think that is necessarily the way to go.

FRANK GIFFORD: Jerry Kramer and I were talking in Washington about his attitude toward the new young players. They are a different type than we were. Oh sure, good athletes with a lot of talent but rich kids, fat kids, who lack the Lombardi kind of dedication. What they're worried about are vacations and investments. And most of them, they have their hand out and they're saying, "What can you do for me now?" Lombardi was football 16 hours a day and he slept only because he had to. The new breed wants to be a 9 to 5 player. It was tough for Vince to accept that type and maybe it would have gotten tougher. But I have the feeling he would have adjusted. His strong mind would have told him he had to.

EDWARD BENNETT WILLIAMS: He was very impatient and intolerant of the kids and their revolutionary ideas. He'd sizzle about long hair and the things that were taking place on campuses. He really didn't see that there was a reason for some of the things that were taking place, or that there was room for a nonviolent revolution in this country. He really felt a certain

George Halas Vince Lombardi

hostility to the tremendous forces of change.

MIKE MANUCHE: He loved to argue. Some things he didn't agree with but he said that he didn't mind if the kids' hair was a *little* long. But he said long hair wasn't practical on a football player. He said hair doesn't change your character and I'd argue with him about that. When he was trying to convince you he did it with his mind rather than the force of his personality. He had great logic.

JIM KENSIL: As he got older, he adapted to things but I don't think he ever mellowed. For example, he wouldn't stand up in front of the Redskins and say that all players should get their hair cut. He would work on them individually. Five years before he'd have stood up and made a speech about it.

JOE BLAIR: So he says to Jerry Smith, "How much do you weigh, Jerry?," and Jerry says, "Oh, 211 or 212, something like that," and Lombardi says, "You should be down to 208 after you get your hair cut. You'll be just right where I want you, at 208." Jerry got his hair cut.

EDWARD BENNETT WILLIAMS: He signed the big ad that appeared to support the President's ABM program. Before that, he came around here with a petition and he said, "Here! Sign here!" and I said, "What? Not me! I'm not going to sign that. I don't think you know what you're signing." He was rather naive politically.

CHUCK LANE: He was a strong advocate of gun control and he had a petition he took around the office and everybody was supposed to sign it. I didn't because I don't believe in gun control. So he and I used to argue about it. He was always getting this goofy mail from people threatening to shoot him and every time he got a letter from one of those guys he'd bring it in and slam it down on my desk and say, "See! See what your friends are trying to do to me!"

BUD LEVITAS: His loyalty always knocked me out. There's this Italian liqueur we handle called Tuaca and it's not very well known in this country. But every time Vince'd go into a place he'd ask for it. When they said they didn't have it he'd bellow, "Well, you better get it because my friend Bud Levitas handles it." He even did that in 21.

BOB SKORONSKI: He talked about that word love, but the way he talked about love was a love of peoples' weaknesses. He used to say, "Everybody can like somebody's strengths and somebody's good looks. But can you like somebody's weaknesses? Can you accept him for his inabilities? That's what we have to do. That's what love is. It is not just the *good* things." He used to stress that.

ETHEL KENNEDY: What was it about Vince that drew me to him? I guess it was because he was so much like Bobby. In a time when so many people seem satisfied to be onlookers or only half-heartedly involved, they lived for entering the arena and once the whistle blew, for them, going flat out became all important. Long hours, hard work and tough decisions were their daily diet. It seems to me that what distinguished Vince Lombardi from other coaches was that he felt so passionately about a game that is in large part emotional. And what raised Bobby above other political figures was his deep-rooted compassion. Perhaps it was because their hearts were so open that both men shared the rare gift of being able to inspire others to perform above themselves.

¶ Perfect specimens never fooled them. It was what lay beneath the surface that fascinated them. Like Larry Brown. He felt he was too small, too young, too inexperienced. And now he's the first to admit that without Vince he would have known the struggle and not the glory. Vince perceived his exceptional drive – the willingness to give 110 per cent – and under his inspiration Larry became one of the league's leading rushers. Bobby had his own Larry Brown in Burke Marshall. When Bobby, as attorney general, interviewed Burke to head the Civil Rights Division at the Justice Department, the two of them just sat there in silence for about four minutes. Finally, Bobby asked, "Do you want the job?," and Burke replied, "I guess so." Burke, with his brilliant mind hidden behind a somewhat forlorn and unassuming exterior, is the most unlikely looking person to head a controversial department of independent, tough-minded lawyers and run it efficiently, imaginatively and with a degree of courage rarely called upon. And yet, somehow, in that silence, Bobby had taken the measure of the man and not found him wanting. Larry Brown was on his way to breaking all the Redskins' records for yardage gained; Burke Marshall made unprecedented gains for Civil Rights.

¶ Both Vince and Bobby knew how to win and how to lose. But, both liked winning a lot better.

¶ Near the end, Vince had captivated, devastated, charmed and dazzled at least one of his legion of admirers. One, whose children now wouldn't dream

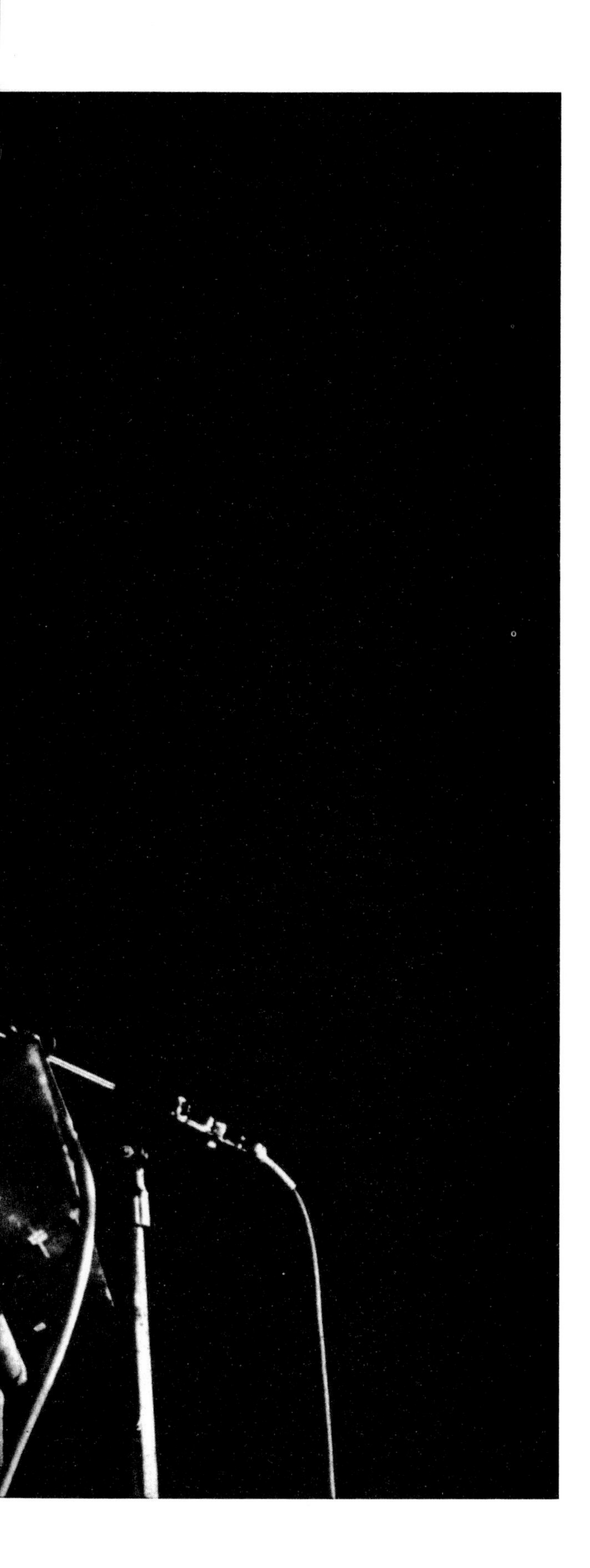

of climbing into their beds without ending their evening prayers with, "... and God bless Vince Lombardi."

HOWARD COSELL: I loved him because of his total absence of hypocrisy. I loved him because he was the best there ever was at what he did. I loved him because he had that curious capacity for making young men responsive to him without their feeling they had been abused.

MIKE MANUCHE: The trouble with men like Vince Lombardi is that people only know one side of them.

Last Days

"What would I do over again if I were given the chance?
Good question.
I guess I would pray for more patience and understanding."

ED BRESLIN: Five or six weeks before he went into the hospital with that first operation we're in Manuche's and he'd just gotten his physical and they've told him he was in good shape. He was really proud. He said, "You ever see a 57-year-old body like this one?" And he stuck out that chest.

TOM BROWN: When I went down to sign my contract in the spring he called me in and he said, "We're really counting on you. We have a shot at winning this thing." So of course I got excited about that and I really went out and worked hard. And then, when I saw him in the hospital bed, I knew there was no way that he would ever coach again. Or maybe even ever get out of bed again. My whole desire, my whole attitude to play, just went boom . . . down.

DAVE SLATTERY: He lost a lot of weight but we thought that was because he was playing golf four days a week. And the night he had a party, June 17 or 18 during rookie camp week, he said to me when we were standing downstairs before dinner, he said to me, "David!," which shocked me and I rushed to him and he said, "Sit down here with me before I fall down." I couldn't believe that.

WELLINGTON MARA: I went down there to Washington on the Fourth of July and we watched the British Open on television, Nicklaus and Sanders in a duel. He told me then that he planned to step aside and help only with the quarterbacks.

OCKIE KRUEGER: When he found out that the owners were meeting in New York he said, "I must go to that meeting. I must go." He said, "If I don't go, they're gonna give in."

WELLINGTON MARA: That final meeting he attended. I'll never forget the speech he made about the threat of a player strike. It was dramatic, not forceful. Maybe it was forceful because of its lack of force. He said, "These are a bunch of 20-year-old kids. We can't turn over to them what so many have built and sweated for." You could have heard a pin drop.

MARIE LOMBARDI: He insisted on going. He was just coming off his first operation then and he had no strength. We had to take along suitcases because we didn't know if we'd have to stay overnight and we had some rain parkas, too. Coming back to the airport it was awful, dragging that heavy stuff. I knew I had to get us through that line quickly – I never asked for favors otherwise – and I went to the counter but the guy there said I'd have to wait.

Vince was gray, ashen gray. It was tragic. We finally got checked in and then we had to carry our bags to the gate. A young man along the way rushed to us and asked if we needed help. Vince only said, "Help me!" And he *never* asked for help.

EARL BLAIK: A day or two before his second operation I called him at home. We had a long chat and he said, "I feel fine now. I'm back down to my playing weight."

FATHER TIMOTHY MOORE: When I went down to Georgetown to see him, he greeted me and then he began to tell me stories. I was not in the mood to hear funny stories because I knew of the seriousness of his illness. I only remember one thing. He asked me, "Tim, what is the easiest way to sink an Italian submarine?," and I said, "I don't know, Vinnie." And he said, "You don't know the easiest way to sink an Italian submarine?"—and he was laughing and I said "No" again—and he said, finally, "Put it in the water!"

VINCE LOMBARDI, JR.: When he was in the hospital he gave the doctors, nurses and orderlies hell. "What's going on around here?" he'd say. There was a resident or intern at the hospital who disliked everyone and he just turned this guy around. A couple of doctors who were on the case and then were off it would come back all the time to see him. And then there was this one doctor who was always talking to the nurses and not bothering with his patients and by the end of the time that my father was there and they couldn't find him they'd ask, "Where is he?," and they were told, "He's in talking to a patient." They couldn't believe that he really had gotten this man to work, to care.

EARL BLAIK: He told me he kept a watch on the people who give him cobalt treatments. He said he counted off the two minutes they were supposed to give him.

PAUL HORNUNG: My hair got pretty long that summer when he was in the hospital and once, near the end, he called me near the bed and he said, "Hey, get a haircut."

MARIE LOMBARDI: He talked in his sleep once about Namath. I just heard his end of the conversation. He was shouting at Namath, telling him to sit down and yelling about how he was a disgrace to football.

ED BRESLIN: We watched that first exhibition together, me and my wife and Marie. They wheeled a television in. Once in the first half Larry Brown carried for about 12 yards but he fumbled and Cincinnati recovered. Vince said, "Oh, shit!" You could see that the game was wearing on him and at the half he said that maybe we'd better go so he could get some sleep. The nurse said that he fell asleep early in the third quarter.

WILLIE DAVIS: It hurt him for players of his to see him in a situation he couldn't control. He was a vain man and all his life he'd believed that nothing was unachievable if he wanted it. I believed that, too, and that's why it was such an emotional thing. He said to me, "Willie, you're one of the finest young men I've ever..." And then he broke off and didn't say more and I left after a minute, maybe two.

MARIE LOMBARDI: His pride was so strong that I think he was embarrassed to see people, his friends, in the hospital. He had lost a lot of weight. I warned them all before they went in but they all wanted to see him. Willie Davis flew all the way from Los Angeles for just a couple minutes in there with him. Then Willie stood in the corridor outside with his head against the wall for half an hour.

WELLINGTON MARA: I called him every day he was in the hospital, at 3 o'clock on the dot.

MARIE LOMBARDI: There were a couple times when Well didn't call right at 3. Vinnie would look at his watch and say, "It's after 3. Where the hell is Well?"

VINCE LOMBARDI, JR.: I was standing in the back of the room and he was talking to my mother. He said, "Come here," and I came up and he said, "The master calls." I thought that he was dying but what he meant was that we always had had that kind of a relationship and he said, "No, I'll be fine." That's all he said and then he fell asleep. That to me was a lot and I think it pretty well explains our relationship. My respect for him got in the way of any other emotion I might have felt for him.

OCKIE KRUEGER: I never realized until those last weeks how really great he was. I mean great in the eyes of the people. When I saw all those wires and cards, the correspondence from the President of the United States down to little kids... well, I just sat down in awe.

BUD LEVITAS: He associated good food and good times with us and those are the things he talked about when we saw him in the hospital. When I went in to tell him we were going for dinner he wanted to know right away where we were going. We told him Duke Zeibert's and that made him happy.

"A great place," he said. Later, when we came back, there was excitement all over the floor. President Nixon had phoned Vince with a get well message. The nurses really were excited. But when we went in to him all he wanted to talk about was our meal and how it was. I tried to change the subject. I said, "I understand you had some excitement around here while we were gone," and he said, "Yeah, but what did you have to eat?" I persisted and I asked him what the President had said. And Vince said, "What do you think he said? He said to get well and everything. Now, did you order the stroganoff like I told you?"

MARIE LOMBARDI: The only time he talked about his condition with any kind of negative attitude was just after he got some flowers from the Hall of Fame people in Canton. He said how nice it was for them to do that and then he said, "I wonder if they'll put me in it now?" There are only two ways of getting in the Hall of Fame – being out of football five years or dying. Normally I'd have said something like, "What the hell did you do that they would put you in the Hall of Fame?" This time I was so shocked I said nothing.

FATHER TIMOTHY MOORE: He said to me, "Tim, I'm not scared to die. I'm not afraid to meet my God now. But what I do regret is that there is so damn much left to be done here on earth."

"I demand a commitment to excellence and to victory and that is what life is all about."

Epilogue

For the Death of Lombardi

I never played for you. You'd have thrown
Me off the team on my best day—
No guts, maybe   not enough speed,
Yet running in my mind
As Paul Hornung, I made it here
With the others, sprinting down railroad tracks,
Hurdling bushes and backyard Cyclone
Fences, through city after city, to stand, at last, around you,
Exhausted, exalted, pale
As though you'd said "Nice going": pale
As a hospital wall. You are holding us
Millions together: those who played for you, and those who entered the bodies
Of Bart Starr, Donny Anderson, Ray Nitschke, Jerry Kramer
Through the snowing tube on Sunday afternoon,
Warm, playing painlessly
In the snows of Green Bay Stadium, some of us drunk
On much-advertised beer   some old   some in other
Hospitals—most, middle-aged
And at home. Here you summon us, lying under
The surgical snows. Coach, look up: we are here:
We are held in this room
Like cancer.
The Crab has you, and to him
And to us you whisper
Drive, *Drive*. Jerry Kramer's face floats near—real, pale—
We others dream ourselves
Around you, and far away in the mountains, driving hard
Through the drifts, Marshall of the Vikings, plunging   burning
Twenty dollar bills to stay alive, says, still
Alive, "I wouldn't be here
If it weren't for the lessons of football." Vince, they've told us:
When the surgeons got themselves
Together and cut loose
Two feet of your large intestine, the Crab whirled up   whirled out
Of the lost gut and caught you again
Higher up. Everyone's helpless
But cancer. Around your bed the knocked-out teeth like hail-pebbles
Rattle down   miles of adhesive tape from hands and ankles
Writhe in the room like vines   gallons of sweat blaze in buckets
In the corners   the blue and yellow of bruises

Make one vast sunset around you. No one understands you.
Coach, don't you know that some of us were ruined
For life? Everybody can't win. What of almost all
Of us, Vince? We lost. And our greatest loss was that we could not survive
Football. Paul Hornung has withdrawn
From me, and I am middle-aged and gray, like these others.
What holds us here? It is that you are dying by the code you made us
What we are by. Yes, Coach, it is true: love-hate is stronger
Than either love or hate. Into the weekly, inescapable dance
Of speed, deception, and pain
You led us, and brought us here weeping,
But as men. Or, you who created us as George
Patton created armies, did you discover the worst
In us: aggression   meanness   deception   delight in giving
Pain to others, for money? Did you make of us, indeed,
Figments   over-specialized, brutal ghosts
Who could have been real
Men in a better sense? Have you driven us mad
Over nothing? Does your death set us free?

Too late. We stand here among
Discarded TV commercials:
Among beer-cans and razor-blades and hair-tonic bottles,
Stinking with male deodorants: we stand here
Among teeth and filthy miles
Of unwound tapes, novacaine needles, contracts, champagne
Mixed with shower-water, unravelling elastic, bloody faceguards,
And the Crab, in his new, high position
Works soundlessly. In dying
You give us no choice, Coach,
Either. We've got to believe there's such a thing
As winning. The Sunday spirit-screen
Comes on   the bruise-colors brighten   deepen
On the wall   the last tooth spits itself free
Of a line-backer's aging head   knee-cartilage cracks,
A boy wraps his face in a red jersey and crams it into
A rusty locker to sob, and we're with you
We're with you all the way
You're going forever, Vince.

James Dickey
February, 1971

Index

The Speakers

The men and women listed below knew Vince Lombardi. Some of them personally, some of them professionally, some of them both. The titles or descriptions listed are, most often, those that applied during the individual's association with Vince Lombardi and the years given are applicable to the same. In many cases a title or position is given in place of the obvious "friend".

The Lombardi Years

Born June 11, 1913; student-athlete, Fordham, 1933-1937; teacher-assistant coach, St. Cecilia's High School, 1939-40; married Marie Planitz, August 3, 1940; teacher-head coach, St. Cecilia's High School, 1941-46; freshman coach, Fordham, 1947; assistant coach, Fordham, 1948; assistant coach, Army, 1949-53; assistant coach, New York Giants, 1954-58; head coach-general manager, Green Bay Packers, 1959-67; general manager, Green Bay Packers, 1968; head coach-general manager, Washington Redskins, 1969-70; died September 3, 1970.

Acknowledgments

This book was conceived in November 1970 by David Boss. It was nurtured through four months of interviews and research. It was written, edited and put together in March and early April of 1971.

There were, inevitably, a lot of helping hands, the largest of which belonged to Steve Taylor, who began the initial series of interviews. In all, he talked with 31 people, many of them players. The results were conversations of sensitivity and technical depth.

Other interview assistance came from Chuck Lane, Lee Hutson and Bob Oates, Jr., the latter interrupting work on his own book, *ProLog: The 1970-71 National Football League Annual.*

Additional photographs came from Nate Fine, who watched Lombardi through the final season in Washington, Herb Weitman, Vic Stein, Malcom Emmons and John Biever, Vernon Biever's son.

A major share of the research was done through newspapers. Information came from: Bob August, *Cleveland Press;* Sam Blair, *Dallas Morning News;* Dave Brady, *Washington Post;* Gary Cartwright, *Dallas Morning News;* John Crittenden, *Miami News;* Arthur Daley, *New York Times;* John Devaney, *Catholic Digest;* Bill Gleason, *Chicago's American;* Milton Gross, *New York Post;* Chuck Johnson, *Milwaukee Journal;* Robert Lipsyte, *New York Times;* Norm Miller, *New York Daily News;* Jack Murphy, *San Diego Union;* Jim Murray, *Los Angeles Times;* Sandy Pawdre, *Philadelphia Inquirer;* Lee Remmel, *Green Bay Post Gazette;* Cooper Rollow, *Chicago Tribune;* Red Smith, *Philadelphia Inquirer;* Francis Stann, *Washington Evening Star;* Gene Ward, *New York Daily News;* Robert Wells, *Milwaukee Journal.*

Help in setting up interviews or obtaining photographs was supplied by: Ed Croke, Roger Hackett, Sid Hartman, Bob Kinney, Vince Lombardi, Jr., Marie Lombardi, Bill McGrane, Marion Rauh and Don Weiss.

The production of the book began with Roz Cole, who either transcribed or supervised the transcription of every major interview. Bob Griffiths was at the Fotosetter machine through all of the book's galleys (more than 80). The proofreading pencils were wielded by Pat Cross, Maxine Patton, Roz Cole, Linda Harlem and Elliott Davis.

The book was designed by David Boss, with assistance from Steven Escalante, and it was placed onto its final boards by Andy Merko, James Selak and Steven Escalante.

There were various people who took the time to reply to questions but whose comments do not appear in this book. They include: Lois Bourguignon, Billy Bidwill, Wally Cruice, William Fetridge, Sid Gillman, Hank Gremminger, Dick Nolan, Carroll Rosenbloom, Ray Scott, William Wallace, Alex Webster and Jesse Whittenton.

John Wiebusch